#323 $15⁰⁰

# *The* Delaware & Hudson Canal

## and it's

## GRAVITY RAILROADS

*Illustrated by the author*

*A history by*
## E.D.LeROY

Copyright 1980.

SEVENTH EDITION 1990

Published by

## WAYNE COUNTY HISTORICAL SOCIETY
### HONESDALE, PENNSYLVANIA 18431

1

# TO ADVENTURERS.

## The completion of the

# DELAWARE & HUDSON CANAL,

has opened a wide and promising field for enterprise, to the Farmer, the Merchant, and the Mechanic.

*This Canal* forms an inland navigation for Boats of twenty-five tons burthen, from tide on the Hudson River, at the village of Bolton, near Kingston, (Esopus) in Ulster County, New York, to the village of Honesdale, in Wayne County, Pennsylvania, a distance of 108 miles.

The Canal now is in successful operation through the whole line, sustaining a respectable and an increasing amount of transportation, which at this time rates at from 250 to 300 tons per day.

## HONESDALE,

is located at the termination of the Canal.

The village plot, which was a heavy and unbroken forest about three years ago, now contains sixty families, and upwards of 100 souls. It is situated in the margin of an extensive region of valuable country, lying northward and westward, over which a multitude of settlements are planted in every direction, although the amount of the present population is small compared with the capacity of the country.

Honesdale is already becoming the depot for an extent of country of more than fifty miles westward and northward.—The Merchant there meets his Goods from New York; and there the Farmer finds a ready market for the products of Husbandry:—and those engaged in subduing the forest, now find an improved value for their timber, acquired by the facilities for transportation.

The face of the country is undulating and hilly, but not mountainous.—The timber, Beech, Sugartree, Hemlock, Ash, &c.—The soil, deep and strong;—much of it produces good crops of Grain, but it excels in the growth of the usual kinds of Grass, for Meadow and for Grazing.

Like most hilly countries, it is well watered and healthy,—and the country is intersected in all directions by Turnpikes and common roads.

## BETHANY,

the County Town of Wayne County, is situated three miles northward from Honesdale, and contains fifty families and upwards of 300 souls.

From the termination of the Canal at Honesdale, a RAIL ROAD is constructed in a western direction, sixteen miles, to the exhaustless Coal beds at Carbondale, on which there is a daily transportation of more than 250 tons.

The Moral and Religious social privileges are good. In Honesdale is an organized Presbyterian Church, and settled Ministry; and a Methodist Society, the residence of a Circuit Preacher.——In Bethany, is a Presbyterian, a Methodist, and a Baptist organized Church. In each is a Bible Society, and in each, and in most of the considerable adjacent settlements, is a Sabbath School and Tract Society.

The facility afforded by the Canal, for a cheap, safe, and expeditious communication with the City of New York, presents to the Farmer, to the Merchant, and to proficients in the various Mechanic Arts, encouragement, which is greatly increased by the consideration that Honesdale, will perpetually be the principal depot and market place, for an extensive region of country, which is now in the commencement of a rapid increase in population and improvement.

The Subscriber offers for Sale, on moderate terms, to actual settlers, a large number of Village Lots, in the Villages of Honesdale and Bethany.—Also, several valuable scites for establishments, for Mechanics and Manufacturers, requiring water power, within a convenient distance from those villages.

And also, a number of Farms with small and large improvements, and upwards of 10,000 Acres of unimproved farm land, among which settlements are interspersed.—The titles are indisputable.

Maps of the Villages, and of the County, may be seen at the office of the subscriber in Bethany, and of John Torrey in Honesdale, where particular information to applicants will be cheerfully communicated.

### JASON TORREY.

Bethany, June 17, 1840

# THE DELAWARE AND HUDSON CANAL

"**M**AURICE, you must hold onto that lot on the Lackawanna that you took for debt from David Nobles. It will be valuable some day for it has stone coal under it." It was Samuel Preston speaking to Maurice Wurts on Market Street, Philadelphia, in 1814. Paul Preston was present and recalled the conversation years later. Whether or not Maurice Wurts was aware of the wealth beneath his land we do not know, but this sound advice may easily have been the foundation upon which one of the greatest private enterprises of the early Nineteenth Century was built.

This enterprise, the Delaware & Hudson Canal, was the result of the industry and foresight of Maurice and William Wurts and their efforts to haul the coal of the Lackawanna Valley to the eastern market.

This is not the place to give a detailed history of the anthracite coal fields, but the fact that anthracite, or "stone coal," existed in the Lackawanna and adjoining Susquehanna Valleys was known as early as 1763, for it is mentioned in the charter granted to the Wyoming Valley settlers by the Connecticut fathers. There is a record of anthracite having been used in 1755 by a gunsmith of Nazareth, Pennsylvania, who, having run out of charcoal, used a quantity of "stone coal" brought him by an Indian in payment for work done on his gun.

## Coal Floated Down River

During the Revolution coal from this locality was floated down the Susquehanna River to the Carlysle Arsenal for use in the manufacture of arms for the American soldiers, but the residents of the valleys of the Susquehanna and Lackawanna Rivers were slow to realize the value of the black stones which lay beneath their farms; even after Judge Fell of Wilkes-Barre made the experiment which he recorded in the fly leaf of one of his books:

"February 11th 1808—

"Made the experiment of burning the common coal of the valley in a grate, in a common fireplace in my home, and found it will answer the purpose of fuel, making a clearer and better fire, at less expense, than burning wood in the common way.—

Jesse Fell"

In the spring of that same year John and Abija Smith floated an arkload of coal down the Susquehanna River to Columbia, but not until the following year did they succeed in inducing some of the residents to buy a few tons.

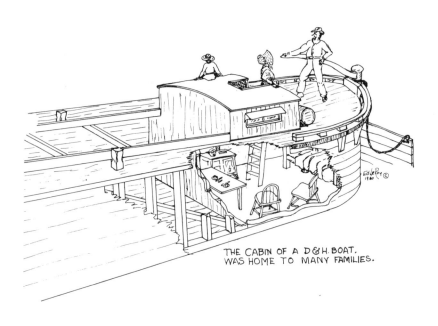

THE CABIN OF A D&H. BOAT.
WAS HOME TO MANY FAMILIES.

These very briefly are the highlights in the history of the North Eastern anthracite coal fields prior to 1814, when the Wurts Brothers began their purchases of coal lands in the Lackawanna Valley.

It appears that David Nobles, a well-known hunter from the Lackawanna Valley, had become acquainted with Maurice and William as early as 1812, during one of their hunting excursions in Wayne County. The improvident Nobles was about to be imprisoned for debt and the Wurts advancing the money to pay the debt, took title to his property on the Lackawanna in return. During 1814 William seems to have taken Nobles into his employ and together they explored a great expanse of the Lackawanna Valley, mapping the coal out-croppings, and purchasing what land they thought of value at from 50¢ to $3.00 per acre.

## Water Route Only Solution

That there was coal in the Valley was evident even to such amateurs as they, but the problem was transportation. The local population was of no consequence and in fact, had little interest in coal with wood so plentiful. Coal laden rafts, or arks, could, without much preparation be floated down the Lackawanna and on down the Susquehanna without great difficulty but the markets which they could reach by that route would hardly be profitable. Their main object was to reach their home town, Philadelphia. Overland transportation, because of its prohibitive cost, was out of the question, and railroads, of course, were a thing of the future. A route by water was the only solution.

4

They mined a small quantity of coal in 1815 and, during the spring of 1816, an attempt was made to float a raft load of this coal down Jones Creek, a tributary of the Wallenpaupack, but fortune was not with them for the raft struck some rocks and was quickly broken up. Although the accounts are somewhat vague and contradictory, they seem to have succeeded in hauling a small quantity over the old Wyoming Road the following year, rafting it down the Wallenpaupack to the falls where it was unloaded, hauled to the Lackawaxen near Paupack Eddy and again loaded on a raft for the long voyage to Philadelphia. Whether or not the raft load ever completed the hazardous voyage is a mystery, but in any event the impracticable Wallenpaupack route seems to have been abandoned in favor of the route through Rixe's Gap and Cherry Ridge to the banks of the Lackawaxen River near the present site of White Mills. A substantial quantity of coal was hauled over this route during the winter months when there was sufficient snow to permit the use of sledges. (Wagons if they had been available could not have been used over the roads which then existed.)

## Shipments Were Small

The accounts vary as to the quantity of coal mined and the quantity actually hauled to the Lackawaxen. It was probably about sixty tons, although some estimate as high as one hundred. However, between 1816 and 1822 a considerable quantity of this coal was successfully rafted to Philadelphia and sold, but there seems to be no record of the total quantity to reach that city, or of the quantity carried on each raft. We know that rafts containing in excess of 20,000 feet of lumber had been going down the Lackawaxen for over half a century and there were many experienced pilots available but then again, managing a lumber raft where the entire load was buoyant was a different matter from handling a raft with a dead weight load of coal.

The many hardships which beset the Wurts brothers do not seem to have discouraged them, for they were ever on the lookout for a better route. In April, 1818, Maurice wrote to Colonel Seeley, of Wayne County, to inquire about the turnpike road he contemplated building through Rixe's Gap to a junction with the Long Ridge Road near the present site of Honesdale. Wurts asked for particular information concerning the practicability of using sledges, and for information concerning spring and fall freshets on the Lackawaxen.

## Canal Route Surveyed

Maurice, while traversing the valley of the Delaware many times, came to know of the broad valley which, in prehistoric times, connected the Delaware and Hudson Rivers. He explored this valley following the Neversink River north, then crossing the Summit he followed Rondout Creek down to the Hudson at Kingston. Here was a route over which a canal might be built enabling them to reach the New York market where they would not have to meet the growing competition of the Schuylkill and Lehigh coal fields.

Maurice undertook a hasty survey of the route to satisfy himself and his brothers that the route was practicable. The residents of the valley, hearing of his plans welcomed him enthusiastically.

5

## 1828–1898

# The Delaware & Hudson Canal
## and the
## Gravity Railroads connecting with the Mines

This great engineering work was the first private enterprise in the United States to cost more than a million dollars. It was constructed to bring the anthracite coal of Pennsylvania to the eastern markets and until well after the civil war, carried most of New York City's coal.

The project was first visualized by Maurice & William Wurts and financed through the influence of Philip Hone, then mayor of New York.

The canal was originally only 3' deep 20' wide at the bottom and 32' at the top. It was finally enlarged to a depth of 6', a bottom width of 32' but the top width was little changed. The original locks were 76' X 9' but were enlarged in 1850 to 100' X 15'.

As the canal was enlarged the tonnage of the boats increased► 1828-10tons, 1840-30tons, 1844-40 1850-140tons. There were 22 aqueducts (4 shown). 136 bridges, 22 reservoirs, 16 dams, 14 feeders.

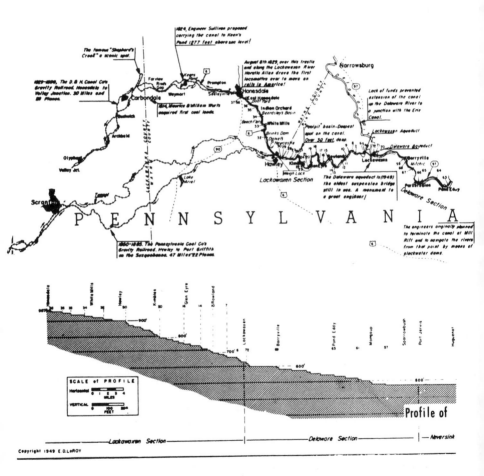

Copyright 1949 E.D.LeRoy

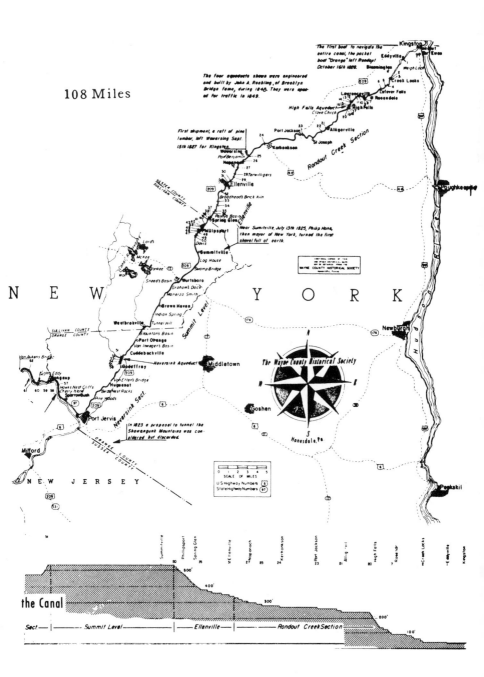

108 Miles

The four aqueducts shown were engineered and built by John A. Roebling, of Brooklyn Bridge fame, during 1848. They were opened for traffic in 1849.

The first boat to navigate the entire canal, the packet boat "Orange" left Rondout October 16th 1828.

First shipment, a raft of pine lumber, left Wurtsboro Sept. 15th 1827 for Kingston.

Near Summitville, July 13th 1825, Philip Hone, then mayor of New York, turned the first shovel full of earth.

In 1823 a proposal to tunnel the Shawangunk Mountains was considered but discarded.

The Wayne County Historical Society

Kingston

N  E  W          Y  O  R  K

N E W      J E R S E Y

SCALE OF MILES
0          1          2          3
US Highway Numbers  6
State Highway Numbers  97

the Canal

Great progress had been made on the Erie Canal and people were aroused to the value of canals. To heighten their interest the Wurts advertised widely in the local papers.

Benjamin Wright had gained great prestige as chief engineer of the Erie Canal when Maurice Wurts approached him with the proposition that he make a detailed survey of their route. Although Wright was unable to come himself he sent two of his younger associates, John B. Mills and Edward Sullivan.

From the survey made by these two men a map was prepared and widely circulated in New York and Philadelphia financial circles. It was a copy of this map that first brought the enterprise to the attention of one of the most influential men of the time, Philip Hone. Hone immediately became interested in the proposition and his name alone gave assurance to others that the venture was likely to succeed.

Shortly before this map was published there was a proposal that the canal be carried through the Shawangunk Mountains in a tunnel and thence across New Jersey. Nothing came of the proposal but it brought forth immediate scathing comments from the Kingston (N. Y.) Plebian, for July 16, 1823, and at the launching of the first boat at Summitville, four years later the hard feeling was revived when a toast was drunk to "the enemies of the D. and H. Canal, like the projectors of the tunneling of the Shawangunk Mountains, may they find their reward in disappointment and their glory in infamy."

## Legal Approval for Canal

While John Wurts did not have the personal magnetism of Philip Hone, he nevertheless was no stranger to politics (he later became a member of the Pennsylvania Legislature). Seemingly without opposition, he obtained from the State of Pennsylvania for his brother Maurice and his heirs and assigns authorization to improve the navigation of the Lackawaxen River. This act was approved by the General Assembly, on March 13, 1823, and on April 23, the State of New York authorized the "Delaware and Hudson Canal Company" to construct a canal from Rondout (Kingston) on the Hudson River to Saw Mill Rift on the Delaware River. The route was to follow up Rondout Creek through the valley to the west of the Shawangunk Mountains, thence down the valley of the Neversink River to the Delaware. At the time no provisions were made for the continuation of the canal beyond that point. However, things were now taking shape and on December 7, 1823, a more thorough survey was begun, likewise under the direction of Benjamin Wright, who was still not free to come himself. This time a more mature man was in the party, which again included Mills and Edward Sullivan. He was Colonel John L. Sullivan, builder of the Middlesex Canal in Massachusetts, who was, according to a pamphlet published at the time, "one of a Board of internal improvement appointed by President Monroe under the late act of Congress," but his enthusiasm for the project, if we can judge from his letters, seems to indicate a more material interest.

On January 7, 1824, Colonel Sullivan reported to Wright that, between the terminus of the canal at Saw Mill Rift and the mouth of the Lackawaxen River, nine dams and locks would be required on the Delaware, and on the Lackawaxen itself at least seventeen dams would be required

## CHAPTER LXI.

## OF THE LAWS OF

## Pennsylvania,

PASSED IN THE SESSION OF

1822—23.

---

*AN ACT.*

To improve the navigation of the River Lackawaxen.

---

**SECT. 1.** *BE it enacted by the Senate and House of Representatives of the Commonwealth of Pennsylvania in General Assembly met, and it is hereby enacted by the authority of the same,* That it shall and may be lawful for Maurice Wurts, of the city of Philadelphia, his heirs and assigns, with his or their surveyors, engineers, superintendants, artists, and workmen, to enter upon the river Lackawaxen, and any one of the streams emptying into the same, that may appear to the said Maurice Wurts, his heirs or assigns, most suitable for the purposes contemplated by this act, to open, enlarge or deepen the same, in any part or place thereof, in the manner which shall appear to them most convenient for opening, enlarging, changing, making anew, or improving the channel, and also, to cut, break, remove and take away all trees, rocks, stones, earth, gravel, sand, or other material, or any impediments whatsoever within the said river Lackawaxen and the branch thereof, which the said Maurice Wurts, his heirs and assigns, may select, and to use all such timber, rocks, stones, gravel, earth, or other material, in the construction of their necessary works, and to form, make, erect and set up any dams, locks, or any other device whatsoever, which the said Maurice Wurts, his heirs or assigns, shall think most fit and convenient, to make a good and safe descending navigation, at least once in every six days, except when the same may be obstructed by ice or floods, from or near Wagner's Gap, in the county of Luzerne, or, from, or near Rix's Gap, in the county of Wayne, to the mouth of the said rizer Lackawaxen, with a channel not less than twenty feet wide and eighteen inches deep, for arks and rafts, and of sufficient depth of water to float down boats of the burthen of one hundred barrels, or ten tuns: *Provided,* That no toll shall be demanded for any boat, vessel or craft in ascending said stream of water, unless the same is converted into a complete slack water navigation, as is authorised by this act.

*(marginal notes:)* Maurice Wurts, his heirs and assigns, authorised to improve the navigation of the river Lackawaxen. Powers. Proviso relative to taking toll.

to make it navigable. It would seem from the Colonel's reference to Keens' Pond that he was even then thinking of an extension of the canal over at least part of the distance. He said in part, "Middle Creek (which enters the Lackawaxen at the present site of Hawley) heads even nearer the mines than Capt. Keens' Pond and may possibly afford a shorter and better route than the west (or main) branch of the Lackawaxen. He also reported that he had made a quick survey of the "South Branch" (the Wallenpaupack) but did not find it favorable.

## Wright Turns to D. & H.

Although Benjamin Wright continued in the service of the Erie Canal, he apparently gave some personal attention to the D. & H. Canal during 1824, and as a result recommended extension of the canal up the Delaware and Lackawaxen Rivers to a point as near the mines as possible. Slackwater navigation on these swift rivers would not, he reported, permit the boats to carry a paying load. Further, owing to the yearly freshets, these dams would have been too costly to maintain but most serious of all, the obstruction which these many dams would have presented to the raftsmen would not have been tolerated by the prosperous and influential lumbering interests, who for the past fifty years had enforced their will upon these valleys. Wright proposed to extend the canal up the Lacka-waxen to the present site of Prompton, thence up Vanorba Brook to Keens' Pond, near the foot of the Moosic Mountains at Rixe's Gap, but Colonel Sullivan, who seems to have been far more enthusiastic than Wright, was all for carrying the canal on over the Mountains directly to the mines. He reported the nearest coal beds to be "within five miles of the proposed head of canal navigation, between which and the coal there is no mountain; the chain being broken by Rixe's Gap, which appeared to me to be about half a mile in width—and it appears to me that if the Lackawanna should not be found capable of feeding a canal through the gap, that the ground would be very favorable to an iron railroad, as they are formed in England." It is evident that this was no passing remark, for he later reiterated "From my knowledge of the place, I am able to say there is no mountainous land intervening between the Lackawaxen and the coal formation and can probably be reached by a continuation of the canal, by feeding from some distance up the Lacka-wanna."

A great deal of confidence seems to have been placed in Colonel Sulli-van, who was an engineer of experience and it seems incredible that he could have made such a misstatement, for the lowest point in the gap was over six hundred feet above Keens' Pond, less than three miles away, and a thousand feet above the mouth of the Dyberry Creek, where the canal finally terminated. Requiring as it did one lock for each twelve feet of rise, it can readily be seen that his proposal was impossible.

## "Hydraulic Lift" Proposed

Sullivan had, if nothing else, a vivid imagination, for as an alternative to continuing the canal across the Moosic Mountains, he favored the scheme of moving the boats directly to the mines over the railroad but his most interesting proposal was his "Hydraulic Lift" which was to do away with canal locks. The "lift" was to be operated by filling or emptying

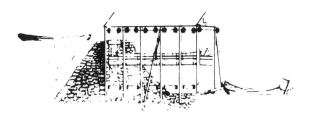

AN OUTLINE of the Lift, shewing the situation of an ascending Boat; the relative distance and elevation of two levels of a Canal. The Transit; the Weights of one side; the Pullies, Axis and Chains also of one side only, that the sketch on this small scale might not appear confused.

known rules of calculation, and being previously *proved*, they are sure to be strong enough : inch iron will suspend 60,000 pounds, or 27 tons. Chain Cables are tested to the extent of 18 tons per inch.

To suspend a boat of 25 tons with tho water, in which she floats, which together with the counterpoise is about 60 tons, four chain cables of one inch iron would be sufficient ; or 16 chains of half inch iron. But in practice, the additional expense of ¼ inch iron, would give 125 per cent more strength to the chains than is theoretically requisite.

The load, whatever it be, necessarily distributes itself over the whole foundation, upon every pillar, to every chain, and with a steady pressure.

The controul or management of the Transit, is principally by levers, which are established in the roof with other apparatus, not necessary now to describe; nor the manner of *compensation* for the transfer of the chains over the pullies.

This improvement will be applicable to elevated districts of country, and to Canals conducted along vallies, where there are mills; when, instead of taking the whole water from them, it borrows only enough for the operation of the Lifts, so small a quantity as scarcely to be a damage. For example, the upper mill pond of a stream, would in the spring, by its redundant water fill the Canal; which would then leave almost the usual quantity to follow its natural course ; thus saving the proprietors a heavy expense, and the neighbourhood of the Canal from the inconvenience of an interruption of a productive branch of business.

J. L. SULLIVAN,
Agent for Mr. Dearborn.

the "transit" in which the boat was carried. He explains that if the boat is to be lowered, it is merely floated into the transit which remained full of water, and thus when the brakes were released the whole thing descended by reason of its own weight. To raise a boat from the lower level the boat was to be floated into the transit, the water allowed to flow out, leaving the combined weight of the boat and transit less than that of the counter balances, causing it to rise to the upper level where water was again admitted and the boat floated out.

Sullivan contended that his "Hydraulic Lift" was best suited for use in mountainous country such as that to be traversed by the new canal. He also argued his lift would conserve water in dry seasons, but there were more conservative men planning the canal and the Colonel and his schemes were soon forgotten.

The Lackawaxen Coal Mine and Navigation Company and the Delaware and Hudson Canal Company, working together, established headquarters in "Sykes' " Hotel and advertised that the charter of the Delaware & Hudson Canal Company "May be *seen* at the bar of the Tontine Coffee House; or if any person should wish to examine it with more mature deliberation than so public a place will admit, he may procure a copy for that purpose, by calling upon a committee of the Lackawaxen Company, at Sykes' Hotel." One pamphlet which was published during 1824 pointed out that the charter granted to the Delaware & Hudson Canal Company by the State of New York was perpetual, but they neglected to point out that the charter granted to the Lackawaxen Company expired in thirty years, at which time the rights reverted to the State with no provision for renewal by the company. This restriction was to cause the managers a great deal of worry in later years, but it was apparently thought best to keep it from the investing public at the time.

## Coal Burning Exhibit

A grate in which anthracite coal could be burned was set up in a fireplace at the Tontine Coffee House and the public invited to come and see the "fine burning qualities of the Lackawaxen Coal" a small quantity of which had been rafted to Philadelphia where it was transferred to the sloop "Toleration," which reached New York City on December 10, 1824.

Subscription books for the purchase of stock in the Delaware & Hudson Canal Company were opened on the 7th of January, 1825, and by two p.m. that day all of the stock had been sold. According to advices given out by representatives of both companies, later in 1824, consolidation of the two companies had also been planned for January 7, but these plans seem, for some reason, not to have been carried out and the merger was not completed until June, 1825, when the Delaware and Hudson Canal Company succeeded to the rights and privileges originally granted to Maurice Wurts.

The Wurts brothers, or the Lackawaxen Coal Mine & Navigation Company, which was the same thing, were to receive $40,000 for the mines and their franchise but this was not paid until late in 1827, at which time they received the equivalent in stock.

# ADDRESS.

—◦◦◦—

NOTICE having been given, that Books will be opened on the 7th of January next, to receive subscriptions to the stock of the Delaware and Hudson Canal Company, it is deemed expedient, on behalf of the Lackawaxen Coal Mine and Navigation Company, at whose instance the chartered privileges of the former company were granted, briefly to lay before the public a few facts and documents, which have not yet been submitted for its consideration.

The charter of the Delaware and Hudson Canal Company having been published, in pamphlet form, in connexion with the Report of Messrs. Benjamin Wright and J. L. Sullivan, it is deemed unnecessary to give it a place among the documents hereto annexed. Those who may wish to examine it, are respectfully referred to the pamphlet above mentioned.* Suffice it to say, at this time, that the charter is perpetual in its duration, and as liberal in its provisions as could be desired. The extent to which the banking privileges may be used in aid of the primary object of the incorporation, will be seen by reference to the Act granting them, which is published herewith.

The above remarks, as to the liberal and comprehensive nature of the charter of the Delaware and Hudson Canal Company, will also apply to the one under which the Lack-

is authorised
of the river
likewise be
ing the Re-
hese several
lvania and
to open a
lson river,
ge, to the
uch terms
ntrol and
sing from

ubscrip-
to the
ny; at
erests,
'e and
Hud-
other
that

the
ore
he

, and furnish ——ing and
an estimate

ery
ac-
have
lying
r that
at the
r-ty of
selves.

ompany
est qual-
by is au-
e Mines,
Pennsyl-
y on the
f the Com-
ry banking
gislature of

body of the
it. It is well
Commencing
rgh, it ranges

---

* This Pamphlet may be *seen* at the bar of the Tontine Coffee House; or if any person should wish to examine it with more mature deliberation than so public a place will admit, he may procure a copy for that purpose, by calling upon a Committee of the Lackawaxen Company, at Sykes's Hotel.

---

It may be proper here to remark, that at the time of the passage of the bill, conferring bank privileges, the Lackawaxen Coal Mine and Navigation Company voluntarily agreed, that the Legislature of New-York might, at its next session, pass a supplement to the charter, fixing the maximum of toll, between the Delaware and Hudson rivers, upon all articles save Coal, at a rate which will average about 50 per cent. above the tolls charged on the Northern and Western Canals. But the tolls upon Coal are to remain as now fixed in the Charter, so that the Company may retain that trade exclusively in its own hands, if it shall see proper.

known to
near the Susquehanna river,

---

* It may not be uninteresting to remark, that the line of the Canal may be so extended, on this route, as to command the trade of the Susquehanna river. The Lackawanock river, which is a fine stream, interlocks with the Lackawaxen, and discharges its waters into the Susquehanna about nine miles above Wilkesbarre. The statute book of Pennsylvania contains an act, authorising an incorporation of a Company to make a Canal, or lock navigation, on the

I N SPITE of the avidity with which the public had subscribed to the stock of the company, there were still many who doubted the practicability of building a canal over such mountainous country. The "Gazateer," a New York City newspaper of the time, commented:

"A good deal has been said among some very enterprising and intelligent persons about a canal making an artificial navigation between the Hudson and Delaware Rivers to bring the coal of the Lackawaxen, a river of Pennsylvania, to the New York market.

"People, generally, doubt the practicability of the proposed route, from the vague ideas of the mountain character of the intermediate country."

Early in 1825 the accompanying estimate for the cost of operation, based upon figures supplied by Benjamin Wright, was published. The figures were somewhat low, probably because they were intended to paint a favorable picture of the prospects in view. They are of particular interest because they do show prevailing wages.

Also early in 1825 John B. Jervis who had gained a great deal of experience on the Erie Canal under Benjamin Wright, became the Chief Engineer of the Delaware & Hudson, and on July 13th, near the present town of Summitville, Sullivan County, New York, Philip Hone, President of the company and mayor of New York, turned the first shovelful of earth in the construction of the D. & H. Canal. Later the same month the first contract, for construction of sixteen miles of canal known as the "Summit Level" were signed. Two other contracts were let that year for construction between the Delaware and Hudson Rivers. Work continued throughout most of the winter and by early spring construction was moving rapidly.

Encouraged by the success of the Erie Canal, the managers had Engineer John B. Mills make a detailed survey up the Delaware Valley from the mouth of the Lackawaxen to Deposit with the expressed purpose of constructing a branch canal northward and then westward to the Susquehanna River and the southern counties of New York State. Benjamin Wright, then Chief Engineer of the D. and H., was of the opinion that the Erie Canal would be inadequate to meet the needs of western towns and what was more, he argued, the D. and H. being further south would have a longer boating season.

Although advocating this branch canal to compete with the Erie, Wright argued against building the D. and H. with a greater prism than originally planned because "smaller boats were easier to handle and speedier."

The "Kingston Advocate" reported twenty-five hundred men and two hundred teams at work in the spring of 1826 and added that more were needed.

Work on the section between Port Jervis and Kingston continued through 1826 and into 1827, and on July 4, 1827, the following bit of news appeared in the Kingston "Plebian:":—

"We last week, mis-stated the information of our informant on the subject of letting water into the canal. We should have said that it was expected that the water would be let into the canal, that day a week this present day. We do think that the occurrence of that event, on this or at all events some day near at hand, very probable, as we know of no obstacle to prevent or retard it."

Water was let into the canal during the first week of July, 1827, and appropriate celebrations were held at Bethany, Wayne County and elsewhere along the line of the canal. But it was soon found that the banks were too porous to hold a boating head of water; also several of the locks were imperfect so that it was not until September that the first freight, a raft of pine lumber consigned to Theron Steel of Kingston, was shipped from Wawarsing, arriving at its destination on Monday, September 17th.

Because the company was unable to lay its hands on the necessary ready cash, the board of managers found it impossible to proceed with the construction of the canal west of Saw Mill Rift until March of 1827, when an additional eight hundred thousand dollars was obtained, over half of which was in the form of a loan from the State of New York. At that time contracts for the Delaware section and the Lackawaxen section as far as "The Narrows" were let, and work immediately begun. In April contracts for thirteen additional miles beyond the Narrows were signed, bringing the part contracted for to within seven miles of Kean's Pond, the planned terminus, but the report to the stockholders concerning the activities for 1827 explains: "It is determined, after much reflection and examination, to stop the canal at Dyberry Forks and from thence to construct a railroad to the coal mines, a distance of fifteen miles nearly."

This same report states that fifty acres of land (owned by Jason Torrey and William Schoonover) were given to the Delaware & Hudson Canal Company by these far-sighted land owners, who retained a like quantity for themselves, "in consideration of the benefits to accrue to the land which they retained." We can infer from this that the gift of land to the company to some extent influenced the choice of a terminus.

Work was plentiful throughout this section of the country at the time and there was some difficulty in obtaining labor, with the result that there was a temporary increase of about 20 per cent in wages over the daily rate of seventy-five cents, but with the importation of more "wild Irish" wages returned to normal.

With the coming of the canal now a certainty, a group of citizens from Wayne County gave serious consideration to the possibility of constructing a branch canal up the Dyberry to a junction with the Lackawanna River parallel to which, the confidently expected, another canal would shortly be built. The plans never went beyond the discussion stage, but during the early days of the canal, the managers were ever hopeful that the State would build a branch canal up the Delaware River from the mouth of the Lackawaxen to bring to the D. & H. the freight of western New York. Benjamin Wright had gone over the ground and reported that "this proposed canal will open a week earlier and close a week later than the Erie Canal. Its route will be shorter and the cost of transportation consequently cheaper."

The signed contracts called for the completion of the entire Lackawaxen section by July, 1828, and the work was pushed to the limit. The records are not specific as to the maximum number of men employed on the Lackawaxen section, but one account states that over six hundred men were at work all winter (1827-1828). The number of wild Irish engaged during the spring and summer of 1828 undoubtedly exceeded that figure by a wide margin and large barracks for housing these men were built near Paupack Eddy (Hawley), and here they soon became the terror of countryside. They were beyond control of the local authorities. They fought with the other laborers and among themselves, but their main enemies were the raftsmen and lumbermen, upon whose domain they were encroaching.

Man for man these two factions were an even match and the dislike was mutual. The raftsmen in particular, had, or at least thought they had, a real grievance against the canal and all those connected with it, for the dam being built across the Delaware below the mouth of the Lackawaxen and the feeder dams on the Lackawaxen itself would interfere seriously with the navigation of their rafts, and then further water drawn from the river to fill the canal would, they contended, so reduce the river level as to make rafting impossible. The canal itself, they thought, would put an end to, or at least seriously injure, their calling. This would have been a severe blow to many people, for during the late 1820's, on the average of seven million feet of lumber were rafted down the Lackawaxen each year. With this in mind we can more easily understand the alarm with which the raftsmen viewed the advance of the canal.

Unfortunately, there are no detailed accounts of these encounters, but Ebeneeaer Scheerer, of Paupack Eddy, a famous Lackawaxen raftsman, claimed to have "cracked a good many Irish skulls" during these early years.

Construction of the canal through the wide flat valley of the Neversink River and upper Rondout Creek was an easy matter compared to the undertaking along the shores of the Delaware and Lackawaxen where the mountains drop abruptly to the river's edge and numerous cliffs rise abruptly out of the river. The blasting was continuous, and in those days, before the invention of dynamite, it was a slow laborious process. It took hours, even days to drill, by hand, one hole which today could be finished in half an hour or less. The steel or iron rods, which were then in use for drilling, were far below present-day standards of hardness and required frequent sharpening. When the blasting hole was finally ready it was partly filled with black gun powder, an uncertain fuse, made of twisted paper, which had been saturated with saltpeter and dried, was inserted and the rest of the hole plugged with not-too-moist clay. When all was ready the "blower" lit the fuse and ran to safety, hoping that, if the fuse did not sputter out, it would fire the powder within a reasonable time. Many were the lives which were lost when a charge hung fire only to explode when the "blower" returned to relight it.

At the foot of Hawk's Nest Cliff, where the mountain walls rise a sheer three hundred feet out of the Delaware River the canal wall, hugging the base of the cliff, was built up forty feet directly from the river bed. Another problem presented itself at the Narrows of the Lackawaxen, where the raftsmen, years before, had blasted away the sixteen foot falls. Here the canal also was built along a sheer rock wall and the embankment was built upon a cribbing of heavy timbers to a height of thirty feet above the river, which here boils through a narrow gorge no more than forty feet wide.

A mile above the Narrows at the mouth of the Tinkwig Brook the river made a sharp "L" turn. To have followed the river would have made it much too difficult for navigation of the boats. A new channel was dug for the river and the canal embankment built across the mouth of the inlet thus formed. The basin or lake created by this hazardous undertaking which was fed by Tinkwig Brook was known up and down the canal as the "Poolpit" and the rumor that this basin had "no bottom"

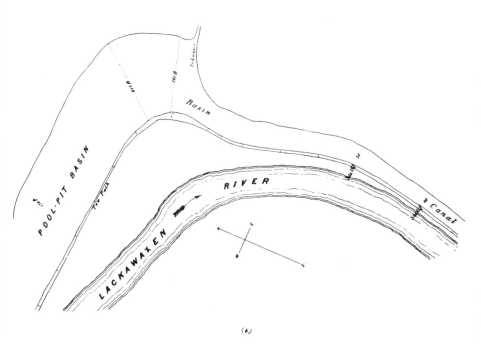

(+)

was widely believed. It is a fact, however, that the bed of this old channel was from ten to sixteen feet below the bed of the new channel, and there the trouble lay, for, as the canal was nearing completion in 1828, this embankment gave way for a considerable distance, causing a flash flood and leaving the river obstructed.

This was the opportunity for which the hostile raftsmen were waiting and they lost no time in presenting to the legislature of Pennsylvania

NARROWS OF THE LACKAWAXEN

their claims that the Canal Company had violated their charter, that the canal embankments were inadequate and that the Delaware dam was improperly constructed so as to make rafting unnecessarily dangerous.

That there were influential interests friendly to the canal is evident from the accompanying reproduction of the rough draft of the resolutions proposed to be published in the local papers of Wayne & Pike Counties to refute the allegations of the rafting interests.

It could not but be conceded that "some individual losses had been sustained" because of this break, and as a result the Canal Company was obliged to settle the claims of various raftsmen.

The break also caused considerable delay in the opening date of the canal, for the embankment had to be rebuilt in a more substantial manner. However, the following article appeared in the Albany "Argus" on October 20, 1828.

"The canal is complete and will be ready for navigation on the whole line in the course of the ensuing week, and the railroad, from the termination of the canal to the coal mines, is in a state of forwardness and will be finished during the present season."

The "Argus" reporter was somewhat behind with his news, for it appears that the packet boat "Orange" had left Rondout on October 16th with many notables on board bound for Honesdale. The "Orange" appears to have been the first boat to navigate the entire canal, and upon its arrival at the new settlement, named in honor of the first president of the Canal Company, the passengers were accorded an elaborate welcome by the local citizens under the leadership of Wayne County's most outstanding citizen, Jason Torrey.

Whereas Memorials have been circulated in this
& the adjacent Counties, addressed to the Legislature
of this Commonwealth Representing that the
Delaware & Hudson Canal Co. have been guilty
of divers transgressions & misdemeanors in violation
of their chartered Rights —

And Whereas from our acquaintance with
the operations of the said Delaware & Hudson
Canal Co. we have every reason to believe
that their conduct has been in perfect consistency
with their chartered Rights, and that, notwithstanding
some individual injuries have been sustained by reason
of a failure of a part of their works upon the
Lackawaxen & by reason of an imperfection in
their dam upon the Delaware, yet we are not
aware that there has been any want of
diligence on the part of the said Co. in
their endeavours to provide a remedy for
these defects & difficulties; & if their works, connected with these things have not yet been brought to
that state of perfection — required by their charter
we have every reason to believe that there will
be no delay on the part of the said Co. but
that all things will be done with the greatest
possible dispatch & with perfect good faith
to the community —

And Whereas the said Memorials have originated with an individual who entertains a
most deadly hostility to the rights of the said
Delaware & Hudson Canal Co. & who it would

seem to gratify his malignity & subserve his own purposes would be willing not only to sacrafice the said Co. but with them the prosp= =erity & dearest rights of an entire community

.And Whereas, the said Memorials, containing charges of a very serious & aggravated characte=, unfounded in fact, have been imposed upon= a large portion of the unsuspecting part of community, who have since discovered the imposition — Therefore

2 Resolved That we view with indignation & disgust, the motives which originated the said Memorials, believing as we do, that our prosperity individually, & as a community is most essentially connected with the existence & successful operations of that Co. which the author of the said Memorials is seeking to prostrate & destroy — And believing also that the said Co. (though they may have failed to gratify the conflicting wishes of individuals) have nevertheless acted with good faith towards the Community generally, & in consistency with their Chartered Rights —

No 4

Resolved That the proceedings of this meeting be signed by the Chairman & Sect & published in the Wayne Enquirer & other papers, in the adjacent Counties friendly to internal improvement

20

PHILIP HONE was not amongst the passengers on the first packet. He was far too busy to spare the time to travel by canal boat, but he did arrive at Honesdale by stage on October 28, 1828, and after viewing the gravity railroad he began the return trip to New York, on horse back, along the tow-path of the canal. He was greatly impressed by "the stupendous rock work" at the Narrows of the Lackawaxen and the dam at the mouth of the Lackawaxen.

Again contrary to the report in the "Argus" the Gravity Railroad from Honesdale to the mines was nowhere near completion although a quantity of coal had been hauled over a hastily finished wagon road through Rixe's Gap to Honesdale where by late November, 1828, there was a sufficient quantity on hand to load ten small boats with ten tons each and start them on their history-making voyage to tidewater.

In the lead of this small squadron was the "Superior" in command of Captain Hickson, followed in order by the "United States" commanded by Captain Cortwright; company boat number two commanded by Captain Lomerau and the "Oliver H. Perry" commanded by Captain Terwilliger. Unfortunately the names of the boats, composing the rest of the squadron, and their captains, have been lost in the passage of time.

As this little squadron passed through the various locks and towns, toasts were drunk to—(and by)—the captains and their crews in celebration of the great event, and as the boats neared the end of the canal the Kingston band, which had come out to meet the flotilla, boarded the "Superior" and "accompanied it to Rondout amidst the playing of appropriate airs." At Rondout the boats were greeted by volleys of musketry fired in salute by the assembled militia following which there was a parade and—of course—many speeches. The orators of the day made many fabulous predictions of the future prosperity of the canal but, few, if any, of those present that day realized how far short of the actual truth these seemingly fanciful predictions fell for not one, of the many who gathered to hear those speeches, could foresee that the canal, even if they could have imagined its final larger proportions, would be completely inadequate to carry the quantity of coal later demanded of it.

## Coal for New York

The ten boats had arrived on December 5, 1828, and on that same day, ten tons of the cargo was transferred to the sloop "Toleration," the same ship which four years before, almost to the day, had brought the first sample of "Lackawaxen Anthracite" to the City of New York by way of Philadelphia. The "Toleration" arrived in New York five days later and part of the cargo was sent without delay to the Western Hotel on Cartlandt Street where a grate had been prepared to demonstrate the great advantages of coal over wood. Later another grate was set up in the company's offices on Wall Street. A part of the first hundred tons to reach Rondout was shipped to Albany for use by Governor Martin Van Buren and members of the Legislature who had been so helpful but although the practicability of anthracite coal as a fuel had by now been conclusively demonstrated, the public was still reluctant to accept the new fuel and so, ironically enough, the canal, which had been built, primarily for the purpose of hauling anthracite coal, hauled far more cord wood than coal during the first two seasons of operation.

Again we have from the Albany "Argus" for December 20, 1828:

"The public scarcely seems aware that a canal 108 miles in length commencing at tidewater, near Kingston, and terminating at the forks of the Dyberry in Pennsylvania (at which place a thriving village is already established called Honesdale), has been completed since October— and this great work has been accomplished principally by the enterprise of an individual company. The first squadron of boats loaded with coal arrived at Tidewater on the 5th instant. Fifty tons have been consigned to Messrs. Townsends of this city which will afford our citizens an opportunity to test its quality."

## Originally Four Feet Deep

The canal as originally constructed was four feet deep, 20 feet wide at bottom and 32 feet wide at the water line. There was a wooden aqueduct 224 feet long over the Neversink River, supported on stone piers, one over Rondout Creek, entirely of stone having two arches one of 50 foot, the other of 60-foot chord. There were in addition ten other smaller aqueducts of varying length, all of wood supported by stone abutments, but the first twenty years of operation there was no aqueduct across the Delaware. In its place the boats were poled across the lake formed by the dam just below the mouth of the Lackawaxen River. After crossing the Delaware they entered directly into the canal and immediately ascended a series of six locks.

Beginning at the tidewater lock at Eddyville the boats passed through Rondout Creek for three miles to the point where the actual canal began. The canal rose through a series of fifty locks to an elevation of five hundred and twenty-five feet above sea level near Phillipsport then continued along at that level for sixteen miles to the Neversink River before descending again fifty-eight feet through a series of six locks to the Port Jervis twelve-mile level. From the western end of this level, at Butler's Falls on the Delaware River, the canal rose to an elevation of nine hundred and seventy-two feet at its terminus in Honesdale. Originally there were in all one hundred nine locks with an average lift of ten feet, although some had a lift of twelve feet, others as little as eight. Each lock was seventy-six feet in length, nine feet in width and the early boats which they accommodated were small, being seventy feet in length and only eight feet seven inches in width.

Contrary to expectations, very little progress had been made during 1828 towards the completion of the Gravity Railroad from Honesdale to the mines and during 1829 further delays developed, so that it was not until October 8, 1829, that the first loaded coal car reached Honesdale. In the meantime the 7,000 tons of coal which were shipped through the canal during 1829 had been hauled over the Rixe's Gap road by wagon and sledge.

When John B. Jervis, then chief engineer for the company, was assigned the task of planning the railroad there were but a few miles of railroad in operation anywhere in the world. In fact four years later, on January 2, 1832, the American Railroad Journal in its first issue gave out the following "list of railroads now constructing, several of which are in part completed and in successful operation:

(1) Baltimore & Ohio, whole length 250 miles, 60 miles completed.

(2) Albany & Schenectady, whole length 16 miles, 12 miles in use.

(3) Charleston & Hamburg, whole length 135 miles, about 20 miles completed upon which the United States mail is carried.

(4) Mauch Chunk, 9 miles completed and in use.

(5) Quincy, near Boston, 6 miles now in use.

(6) Ithica & Owego, 29 miles.

(7) Lexington & Ohio, 75 miles.

(8) Camden & Amboy, 50 miles.

(9) Lackawaxen, 16 miles."

(The last named was the D. & H. Gravity.)

The locomotive had yet to make its appearance in this country, nevertheless, the following optimistic article appeared in the Dundaff, Pa., "Republican."

December 20, 1828: "The railway is to be furnished with five stationary engines and seven locomotive steam engines. It is estimated that the railway and its appendages will transport 540 tons per day in one direction. The steam engines were taken up as soon as the canal was navigable and it is expected that the railway will be in operation as early as June next."

The steam engines "taken up" were, of course, the stationary engines for use at the heads of the planes.

There was great activity at the head of the canal late in 1828 and during 1829 for, while we do not know the number of men and teams engaged in hauling coal, the number must have been considerable, and the village of Honesdale had begun to grow rapidly, for we read in Hazard's "Register," Philadelphia, February 28, 1829:

"Honesdale is situated in the Lackawaxen Valley at the confluence of the Lackawaxen River and Dyberry Creek three miles and a half southeast of Bethany. Two years ago the site of the village was occupied by woods, but since the commencement of active operations near the head of the Lackawaxen Canal and on the railroad, both of which terminate near this place a town has been laid out on this spot and now contains 18 dwelling houses, four stores, a tavern, a post office and the offices of the Delaware & Hudson Canal Co."

## "The Gravity"

As we have said, the only railroads which existed were in the earliest experimental stage when John B. Jervis undertook the building of the D. & H. Canal Company's Gravity Railroad or, as it became more familiarly known locally, "The Gravity." Steel or even soft iron rails were unknown then, so the road as Jervis originally built it consisted of 6 x 12 inch stringers of hemlock set on edge to form the rails. These stringers which were twenty to thirty feet in length were notched into heavy cross ties to which they were secured by wooden pegs. The cross-ties were placed ten to fifteen feet apart and were in turn supported by wood or stone piers and thus the whole structure was held clear of the ground to prevent rotting. The running edge of the rails was protected from wear by a strip of strap iron one-half inch thick by two and one-half inches wide and was secured to the rails by countersunk screws.

The planes on the original gravity road had double parallel tracks whereas the single tracked levels were provided with sidings. Actually there were no "levels" on the road, the term being only relative for while the grade on the planes was extremely steep, there was a slight grade on the levels favoring the loaded cars so that it was necessary to haul the empties back by mules or horses. Each horse hauled five cars, one of which was the car in which he rode as the train was returning by gravity.

Beginning at an elevation of 1,200 feet at Carbondale, the "Gravity" rose to an elevation of 1,907 feet at Rixe's Gap through a series of five planes and the intervening levels. The road then descended the east side of the Moosic Mountains by three planes and levels to an elevation of 985 feet at Honesdale. The planes were numbered eastward from Carbondale. Numbers 1 to 5 being on the west side of the ridge; 6, 7, and 8 on the east.

Stationary steam engines were located at the summit of each of the first five planes. Each engine operated two huge drums placed in tandem, being eight feet in diameter and having a flanged rim nine inches wide: Around each pair of these drums a huge chain made three turns thence passing to the foot of the plane where it was attached to a trip of loaded cars. The other end of the chain was attached to a like number of empty cars being lowered which acted as a counter balance and thus left only the dead weight of the coal to be overcome by the hoisting engine. Only one of the drums was geared to the engine, the other acted merely as an idler helping to create friction and prevent the chains from slipping.

On planes 6, 7 and 8, where the loaded cars were descending, no motive power was required. A braking system was provided, consisting of two drums similar to those of the powered planes but connected merely to a heavy brake.

Considering the lack of experience with such contrivances, the hoisting engines and drums seem to have been a reasonable success, but the chains were an absolute failure and were discarded in favor of ropes after having been in use only a few months during 1829. Concerning them, Dr. Benjamin Sillman wrote to Mr. Hazard of Philadelphia during July, 1830:

"Last year there was much inconvenience from chains by which the steam engines draw up the coal wagons from the mines; during the season about fifty coal wagons were dashed to pieces in that manner, and when chains parted the wagon could not be seen in its descent; so instantaneously did it dart to its goal, that only a dim streak could be traced through the air. They now use cables of hemp and the accidents do not any longer occur."

On December 12, 1830, John Bolton, the president of the company, wrote to the Governor of New York a letter in which he said:

"Our railway has fully met our expectations, since the substitution of ropes for chains on the planes. The change, however, which was effected at the close of winter was very expensive."

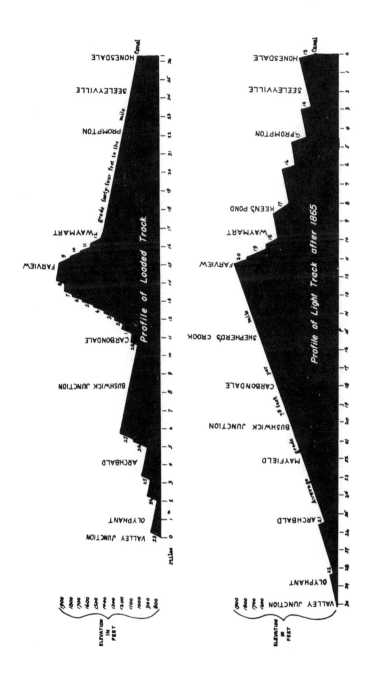

Profile of Loaded Track.

Profile of Light Track after 1865

HONESDALE · Canal
SEELEYVILLE
PROMPTON
Grade twenty-four feet to the mile
WAYMART
FARVIEW
CARBONDALE
BUSHWICK JUNCTION
ARCHBALD
OLYPHANT
VALLEY JUNCTION

HONESDALE · Canal
SEELEYVILLE
PROMPTON
KEENS POND
WAYMART
FARVIEW
SHEPHERD'S CROOK
CARBONDALE
BUSHWICK JUNCTION
MAYFIELD
ARCHBALD
OLYPHANT
VALLEY JUNCTION

ELEVATION IN FEET
1900 1800 1700 1600 1500 1400 1300 1200 1100 1000 900 800

ELEVATION IN FEET
900 800 700 600

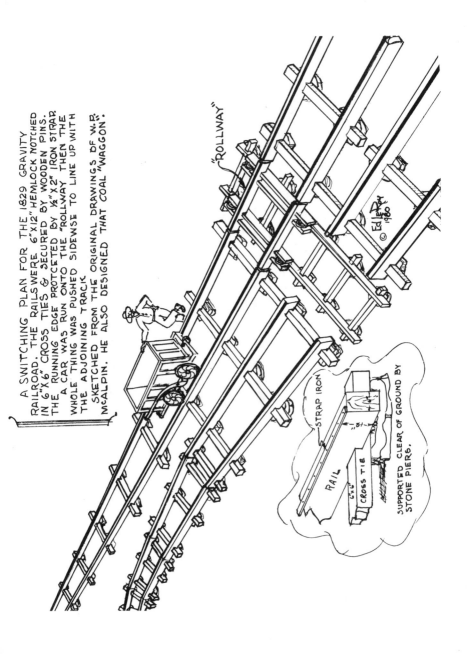

A SWITCHING PLAN FOR THE 1829 GRAVITY RAILROAD. THE RAILS WERE 6"x12" HEMLOCK NOTCHED IN 6"x6" CROSS TIES & SECURED BY WOODEN PINS. THE RUNNING EDGE PROTECTED BY ½"x2" IRON STRAP A CAR WAS RUN ONTO THE "ROLLWAY" THEN THE WHOLE THING WAS PUSHED SIDEWSE TO LINE UP WITH THE ADJOINING TRACK.

SKETCHED FROM THE ORIGINAL DRAWINGS OF W.R. McALPIN. HE ALSO DESIGNED THAT COAL "WAGGON".

"ROLLWAY"

STRAP IRON

RAIL

CROSS TIE

SUPPORTED CLEAR OF GROUND BY STONE PIERS.

Expensive they must have been and cumbersome also for these ropes measured seven and one-half inches in circumference. To protect this investment the ropes, although they were bound with cords and heavily tarred, were carefully taken in each Saturday night and not brought out again until Monday morning for the "Gravity" like the canal, did not operate on Sunday.

The ropes, while they greatly lessened the danger of runaway cars brought a new difficulty in that they were frequently slipping on the drums, particularly when they were wet and not until the expedient of connecting the idler drum to the driven drum, by means of a rope belt, was struck upon, did they overcome to a great extent this difficulty although that danger remained until years later when the huge ropes were replaced by the first steel cables made by John Roebeling.

The grade on the "levels" ranged between twenty-four and forty-four feet to the mile and here again the company met another difficulty for, as the name of the road implies, the cars were allowed to descend by gravity and their speed had to be controlled. Various schemes were tried, amongst them being an elaborate windmill affair, connected to the axles by ropes or belts and retarding the speed by friction. Of this contraption a contemporary wrote "it is a new and ingenious application, by Chief Engineer Jervis, of a known power, to the descending levels, which may well deserve the name of an invention." This idea was soon discarded and a simple brake using the pressure of a bent sapling applied directly on the wheels came into general use.

The next improvement on the railroad was the addition of a 2 x 4 oak strip to the running edge on top of the original hemlock rails which were soon found to be too soft. The protecting strap iron was replaced on top of the oak and this arrangement served for many years.

During 1828 a young engineer, Horatio Allen by name, had become associated with the D. & H. and with Engineer Jervis, who was then planning the gravity railroad. This connection led to his being chosen in the fall of 1828 to go to England to arrange for the purchase of four "locomotive engines" for use on the "Gravity" planes.

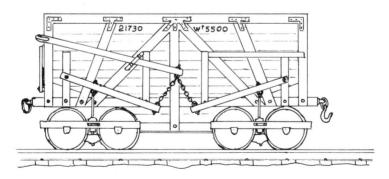

BUILT OF PLANKS, GRAVITY CARS CARRIED 2.75 TONS OF COAL.

It should be observed that when Mr. Allen arrived in England the use of the multitubular boiler in locomotive engines was unknown, or was only talked about. In the engraving of the Killingworth engine in Wood's "Treatise," he shows and describes an exhaust-pipe which " is opened into the chimney, and turns up within it ;" but the value of the steam blast was then not recognized. The locomotives which were known in America at that date were those which have been described. It is therefore not remarkable that Mr. Allen, then only 27 years of age, and feeling the responsibility of his position, should be governed by the instructions which he received when he left home. He therefore ordered of Messrs. Foster, Rastrick & Company, of Stourbridge, three locomotives of the Stockton & Darlington type.* One of these (fig. 1) was the engine that afterward had the distinction of being the first one that was ever run in America. It had four coupled wheels,

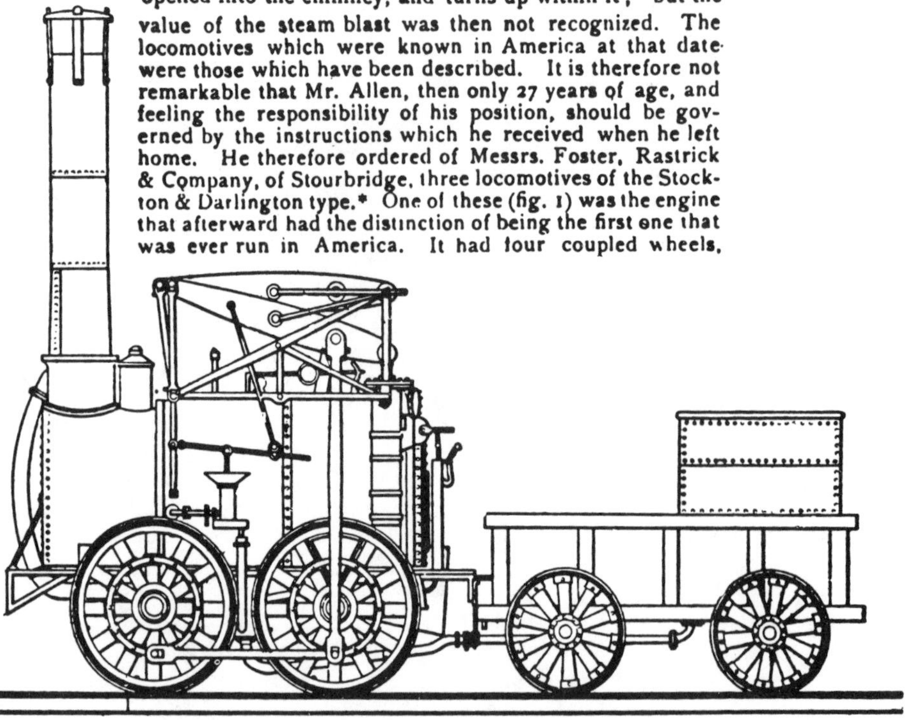

FIG. 1.—" STOURBRIDGE LION." 1828.

all drivers, driven by two vertical cylinders, with 36-in. stroke, placed at the back end and on each side of the boiler. The motion of the piston was transferred through two grasshopper beams above the cylinders, and from those beams by connecting-rods to the crank-pins on the wheels. The front end of the beam was supported by a pair of radius rods which formed a parallel motion. The spokes of the wheels were heavy oak timbers, strengthened by an iron ring bolted to the spokes midway between the hub and felloes, and the latter was made of strong timber capped by a wrought-iron tire. From the illustrations of this engine which have survived, the cranks on each pair of wheels were apparently at right angles to each other, other-

* In the latter part of his life, Mr. Allen was of the impression that one locomotive was ordered of this firm and two of Messrs. Stephenson & Co., of Newcastle, but an examination, since his death, of some correspondence on file in the office of the Delaware & Hudson Canal Company has shown conclusively that three engines were built by the first-mentioned firm and one by the Messrs. Stephenson. This correspondence shows that the locomotive built by the Stephensons arrived in New York on board the ship " Columbia" about the middle of January, 1829. The first one of those, built by Foster, Rastrick & Co., arrived on board the " John Jay," May 13, of the same year; the second one on the ship " Splendid," about the middle of August, and the last one on September 17, on the " John Jay."

wise it is not clear how the engine could start when they were on one of the dead points  The boiler was cylindrical and had several large flues inside.

After Mr. Allen arrived in England, as already stated, he made the acquaintance of George Stephenson, and from him received much valuable aid and advice.  He visited Liverpool, the Stockton & Darlington Railway, and Newcastle.  Locomotive engines had then been in successful use since 1814, and the subject of railroads was attracting great attention, not only in that country, but in America and the whole civilized world as well.

On his arrival in England Mr. Allen found, as Mr. Wood, in the preface to his treatise says, that " The eyes of the whole scientific world were upon the great work of the Liverpool & Manchester Railway ;" and as another writer of that period reported, "discoveries were daily made of new principles applicable to locomotives, and, extraordinary as they now are, in their power and velocity, great improvements may yet be reasonably anticipated." In England Mr. Allen spent considerable time in visiting the different roads then in operation, and in studying the performance of the locomotives in use.  The kind of power to be used on the Liverpool & Manchester Railway was regarded as a question of great moment.

Mr. Allen made a contract with Messrs. Stephenson & Company, of Newcastle, for one more locomotive.  This engine, he said, was ordered to be identical in boiler, engine plan, and appurtenances to the celebrated *Rocket*.

When completed the four engines were shipped to New York and arrived there during the year 1829.  The *Stourbridge Lion*, it is said, was sent from the foot of Beach Street, in New York, to Rondout, and thence reshipped by canal to the track at Honesdale, where it made its celebrated first trip.  Some of the other engines were for a time stored in the warehouse of Messrs. Abeel & Dunscom on the East side of New York.  One of them was there raised up so that its wheels were not in contact with the ground and was exhibited in motion with steam on as a curiosity to the public.  The singular part of this is that it is not now known what ever became of these engines. All trace of them has been lost as completely as though they had been cast into the sea.

Why the *Stourbridge Lion* was sent to Honesdale and not the Stephenson engine, which arrived in New York first, is not known.  If this one, which has since passed into oblivion, had been selected for the first run we would have had the remarkable circumstance that a trial of an engine, which Mr. Allen said was built on substantially the plan of the famous *Rocket*, would have occurred in this country *before that* celebrated event took place in England.

" It is to be regretted," said Mr. Allen, " that one of the Stephenson locomotives was not sent, and for the reason, that they were the *prototypes* of the locomotive *Rocket*, whose performance in October of the same year so astonished the world.  If one of the two engines in hand ready to be sent had been the one used on August 9th, the performance of the *Rocket* in England would have been anticipated in this country."*

The story of this first trial of the *Stourbridge Lion* has often been told.  The engine received its name, Mr. Allen said, " from the fancy of the painter who, finding on the

29

boiler end a circular surface, slightly convex, of nearly four feet diameter, painted on it the head of a lion in bright colors, filling the entire area."

The river and canal being closed by ice, it was not until the opening of navigation in 1829 that access was had to the railroad at Honesdale, Pa., which was then at the head of the canal and at the beginning of the railroad.

Being at liberty during July and August, Mr. Allen volunteered to go to Honesdale and take charge of the transfer of the locomotive from the canal-boat to the railroad track. Of the place where the trial was made he wrote :

" The line of road was straight for about 600 ft., being parallel with the canal, then crossing the Lackawaxen Creek, by a curve nearly a quarter of a circle long, of a radius of 750 ft.,on trestle-work about 30 ft. above the creek, and from the curve extending in a line nearly straight into the woods of Pennsylvania.

" The road was formed of rails of hemlock timber in section 6 × 12 in., supported by caps of timber 10 ft. from center to center. On the surface of the rail of wood was spiked the railroad iron—a bar of rolled iron 2¼ in. wide and ¼ in. thick. The road having been built of timber in long lengths, and not well seasoned, some of the rails were not exactly in their true position. Under these circumstances the feeling of the lookers-on became general that either the road would break down under the weight of the locomotive, or, if the curve was reached, that the locomotive would not keep the track, and would dash into the creek with a fall of some 30 ft.

" When the steam was of right pressure, and all was ready, I took my position on the platform of the locomotive alone, and with my hand on the throttle-valve handle, said : ' If there is any danger in this ride, it is not necessary that the life and limbs of more than one should be subjected to danger,' and felt that the time would come when I should look back with great interest to the ride then before me.

" The locomotive having no train behind it answered at once to the movement of the valve ; soon the straight line was run over, the curve was reached and passed before there was time to think as to its being passed safely, and soon I was out of sight in the three miles' ride alone in the woods of Pennsylvania.

" I had never run a locomotive nor any other engine before. I have never run one since, but on August 9th, 1829, I ran that locomotive three miles and back to the place of starting, and being without experience and without a brakeman, I stopped the locomotive on its return at the place of starting. After losing the cheers of the lookers-on, the only sound, in addition to that of the exhaust steam, was that of the creaking of the timber structure.

" Over half a century passed before I again revisited the track of this first ride on this continent. Then I took care to walk over it in the very early morning, that nothing should interfere with the thoughts and the feelings that, left to themselves, would rise to the surface and bring before me the recollections of the incidents and anticipations of the past, the realization of the present, and again the anticipations of the future.

" It was a morning of wonderful beauty, and that walk alone will, in time to come, hold its place beside the memory of that ride alone over the same line more than fifty years before."

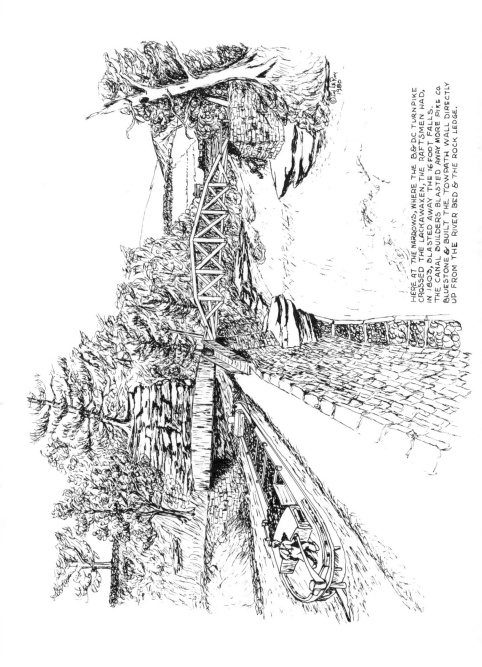

HERE AT THE NARROWS, WHERE THE B&DC TURNPIKE CROSSED THE LACKAWAXEN, THE RAFTSMEN HAD, IN 1803, BLASTED AWAY THE 16 FOOT FALLS. THE CANAL BUILDERS BLASTED AWAY MORE PIKE CO. BLUESTONE & BUILT THE TOWPATH WALL DIRECTLY UP FROM THE RIVER BED & THE ROCK LEDGE.

"Stourbridge Lion" was never again used on rails and for a while it lay stored in a shed in Honesdale, then it was dismantled, the boiler taken to Carbondale, where it was used in the company shops and later sold, but the original engine has now been re-assembled and partly reconstructed and is housed in the Smithsonian Institution in Washington, D. C.

A word here about Horatio Allen would not be out of place for he was one of the outstanding civil engineers of his time. In addition to having the honor of being America's first locomotive engineer he built the famous reservoir at 42nd Street and Fifth Avenue in New York where the Public Library now stands. Another of his achievements was the construction of High Bridge which carried the Croton Aqueduct across the Harlem River to New York City. A few years later he became chief engineer of the Erie Railroad and in 1846 was elected its president. He died in East Orange, N. J., on January 1, 1890.

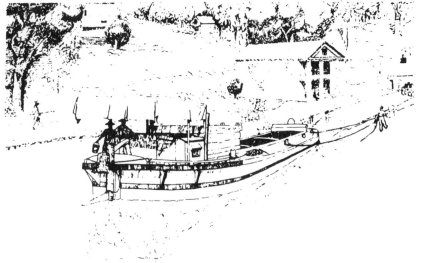

The D&H Canal

In December, 1829, when freezing weather brought the first full year of operation of the Canal to a close, the prospects for the following year seemed to be good but, unfortunately, some of the coal which had been sold on the New York market had been of such poor quality that the standing of the company was seriously prejudiced. As a result only forty-three thousand tons were sold during 1830, far from the company's expectations and, when in 1831, the increase, while better, was again not what had been expected, the managers began to make efforts to interest the New England market.

In April of 1830 the "Wallenpaupack Improvement Company" was incorporated by the State of Pennsylvania. This company, which seems to have had only local backing, proposed to construct a railroad from the mines near Slocum Hollow (Scranton) on the Lackawanna River to "the forks of the Wallenpaupack," a distance of sixteen miles, and from that point a canal or series of slackwater pools to the head of the falls at Wilsonville, a distance of about eighteen miles, according to their calculations. From Wilsonville, they proposed to construct a gravity railroad down the steep hillside, crossing the Lackawaxen River on a trestle to a junction with the D. & H. at Paupack Eddy. The cost of operating over such a route could be prohibitive for the cargo would have had to be handled four times en route. First after being loaded onto gravity cars at the mine the coal would have had to be transferred to canal boats from which, upon reaching Wallenpaupack Falls, it would again have to be laboriously shoveled into the second gravity cars for the mile-and-a-half trip down to the D. & H. Finally because the early D. & H. boats were not seaworthy enough to venture regularly upon the Hudson River a transfer would be necessary at Rondout.

It seems fortunate for those who might have invested in the scheme that these plans never materialized.

In spite of the difficulties and the setbacks which the company had undergone, President Bolton, in a letter written December 12, 1830, said:

"As a measure of economy, time was taken last spring to put the canal in the best possible condition, which deferred the opening until the 20th of April and the very slight interruptions which have occurred in the navigating proves the good judgment of our chief engineer, Mr. Jervis—it has now become a substantial work and all exposed parts have been well secured. They have recently been subjected to a very severe test as a heavy fall of snow was succeeded by several days of incessant rain. The Delaware and Lackawaxen Rivers rose with great rapidity. The former, at our crossing place, twelve feet in twenty-four hours but the only injury sustained was on the Lackawaxen by water passing through a slope wall and washing some of the bank into the canal which was repaired at an expense of $15.00. This detail is given in consequence of doubts having been expressed of the stability of our work in an official memorial to the legislature in 1829."

With reference to the cost of repairs which Mr. Bolton mentioned, it is safe to say that the cost of the same work today would exceed $200.

### Rivalry With Raftsmen

We have in this letter a reference to the old antagonism with the raftsmen and it is in this connection that the copy of the final draft of the resolutions dated February, 1830, is of interest. The controversy between the D. & H. and the raftsmen had now become so serious that Philip Hone was called upon to lay aside his affairs and go to Honesdale where he arrived February 15, 1830, and the following day set out in a cavalcade of fifty persons representing both factions as well as the Pennsylvania Legislature. They proceeded along the tow path, following the Lackawaxen River to the Delaware, viewing the alleged obstructions as they went.

The following day Hone and his party returned to Honesdale along the towpath while the legislative party returned to Harrisburg by way of the lower Delaware but it was fortunate, Hone records in his diary, that the rafting interests returned by a different route for their leader, a Mr. Meridith, had been hung in effigy at several points. As a result of this trip it was determined that the claims of the raftsmen were baseless for the navigation of the Lackawaxen had been improved rather than impeded.

Buckingham. Febr 8th 1830

At a public meeting held at the House of John Lords, Junr.
on the part of Manchester and Buckingham we unanim-
ously agree to the propositions within mentioned
and the chairman and secretary sign the same

John Lord Chair.

William Adams secry

A proposition was produced to the meeting from
John B. Jervis Esquire the Chief Engineer of the
Delaware & Hudson Canal Company, agreeing on
the part of said Company, that those interested in
the rafting navigation of the Delaware & Lackawaxen
rivers, may choose a Committee to superintend
and make such improvements upon the aprons
of the dams as they shall deem necessary at
the expense and under the responsibility of the said
Canal Company. —

Therefore conceiving that the said proposition
ought to be received by those interested in the
rafting navigation, as satisfactory for the present
in relation to the improvement of the state of the dam.

Resolved that Jacob W. Welch
be and are hereby appointed Delegates from this
meeting to meet such Delegates as may be
appointed by other Townships meetings, at the
Court House in Bethany on the evening of Tuesday
the 9th instant for the purpose of associating the
views of the Lumber interest on the subject
and of making a suitable representation
thereof to the Legislature. —

To add to the worries of the builders of the new canal the Legislature of the State of New York chartered the Hudson & Delaware Railroad on April 19, 1830, to be built from Newburgh to Carpenter's Point (Port Jervis) from which point it was to cross into Pennsylvania and continue up the Delaware and Lackawaxen Rivers passing through Cobb's Gap which, their engineers reported, was "300 feet lower than Rix's Gap, the pass over which the railroad of the Delaware and Hudson Canal Company is carried." By this route, they claimed, a load of coal could reach New York City in twenty-four hours. Fortunately for the D. & H. the road was never built and no competing railroad entered the Lackawaxen Valley until thirty-five years later.

The D.&H. Canal ∽ THE LIGHT BOAT, RIDING HIGH OUT OF WATER, HAS STEERED TO THE BERM BANK OF THE CANAL AND ITS TEAM HAS HALTED SO THAT THE TOW-LINE HAS SUNK TO THE BOTTOM ALLOWING THE LOW-LYING LOADED BOAT TO PASS. GILSON'S LOCK IS AHEAD. BEYOND THE TOW-PATH IS THE DELAWARE AQUEDUCT

THE value of canals as means of transportation had by now been proved beyond any doubt and there were yet many people who could not be convinced that railroads would ever be practicable for distances of more than a few miles. In any event the backers of the aforementioned railroads could not have been encouraged by a lengthy article written by W. R. Hopkins, a prominent engineer, for the Albany "Evening Journal" October 15, 1830. In it he said,

> "There are places enough to make railroads where water can not be had for canals and to such places they should be confined. I am opposed to seeing the streams of our State run idle and the spirit of an enlightened canal policy swept away by railroad fanaticisms."

That the economy of transportation by canal cannot be questioned, when the element of time is not of great importance, will be evident from the following table of tolls published for 1831:—

*(The amounts shown are per ton per mile)*

| Salt | 2½ cents | Liquor, Sugar, Molasses | 1 cent |
|---|---|---|---|
| Cement | 3½ cents | General Merchandise | 3 cents |
| Ground Tanners bark | 2 cents | Iron, up the Canal | 3 cents |
| Unground Tanners bark | 1½ cents | Iron, down the Canal | 2 cents |

*Timber in boats per 100 cu. feet per mile but not to exceed total amount shown for any distance on the canal—*

| Hemlock | 1 cent ($.75) | Pine | 1½ cents ($1.00) |
|---|---|---|---|
| Oak | 2 cents (1.50) | Maple-Popler | 3 cents ($3.00) |

*Timber in rafts properly secured, No maximum.*

| Hemlock | 2 cents | Pine | 3 cents |
|---|---|---|---|
| Oak, Maple, Popler, etc. | 4 cents | | |

Cord wood in boats, from 1 to 10 miles, per cord per miles, 4 cents. Above 18 miles, 60 cents per cord, plus 1 cent per cord for every five additional miles.

Mileage on boats down the canal, 2 cents; up the canal, 4 cents.

The franchise granted the canal company would not permit charges in excess of 4 cents per ton per mile except on coal.

At no time during the first twenty years of operation did the tolls from the various commodities exceed $50,000, although the tonnage of the company's coal shows, with a few exceptions, a regular but gradual increase.

The Canal had opened up a new, cheap means of transportation for the residents of Wayne and Pike Counties and heavy items, on which the freight charges had, in many cases, exceeded the value of the article, were now brought within the means of the average farmer. Obviously the traffic on the Canal was not limited to coal, although coal always remained the one important item. Durham boats were sometimes seen upon the D & H for on December 18, 1830 the Manch Chunk Currier reported that two, the "Pilot" and the "Spy" had arrived at that place from—

"Honesdale at the head of the Delaware & Hudson Canal—to Carpenter's Point, at which place they took on 15 tons of plaster of Paris. Three miles below the Water Gap they took on a cargo of boards for Bethlehem on the Lehigh, 12 miles above Easton, then in ballast to this place in ten days. A. Bently, master of the boats, says he has been in cannalling business for several years and intends to build two deck boats for the coal trade next season."

A still stranger sight must have been witnessed when, according to the Milford Eagle for August 6th, 1831,

". . . two Tuscarora Indians with their squaws and papooses arrived at this place, Friday last, by water, in bark canoes in which they travelled from Buffaloe by way of the Erie Canal to the North River & from that river into the Delaware & Hudson Canal and so into the Delaware River, a short distance above Carpenter's Point. They are shortly to leave for Pottsville in this state."

On April 13, 1831 John Wurts was elected president to succeed John Bolton, who had held that office since Philip Hone had resigned in 1826. Wurts seems to have been a capable man and what is more his qualifica-

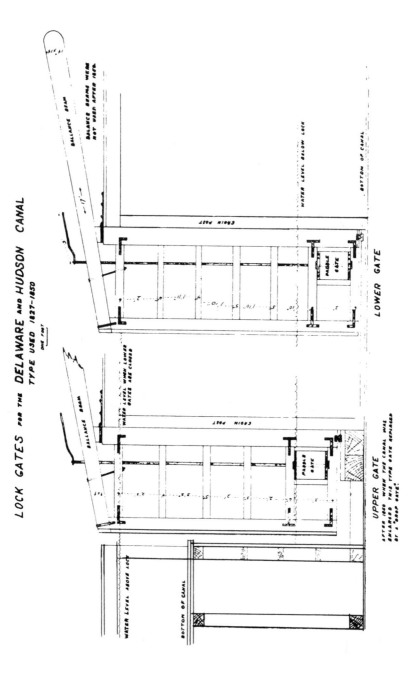

LOCK GATES for the DELAWARE and HUDSON CANAL
TYPE USED 1827-1850

37

tions as a lawyer were of great value to the company. Partially as a result of his policy of retrenchment the company gradually assumed a more secure financial footing and the stock which had begun to decline, after the failure of the "Stourbridge Lion" showed new strength but this period of prosperity was not to last long for during the second administration of President Jackson the speculating public seems to have lost confidence in such investments and the stock which had reached 125 in the fall of 1833 took a precipitous drop during the last part of that year to 75. Hone in his diary remarks "What will be the end of it God only knows and General Jackson don't care." 1834 was a decidedly poor year for the company, as well as for business in general, but the following three years showed a gradual improvement. However, along with the rest of the nation the D & H suffered a setback during the financial panic of 1837. The results were most severely felt the following year when slightly more than 76,000 tons were shipped through the canal as compared to the previous high of 115,387 tons.

As has previously been described, the earliest boats to pass through the canal carried only ten tons each. A quantity considerably below their actual capacity because, in spite of the glowing accounts describing the canal as "having been executed in the most permanent and perfect manner" it was not until 1839 that the full head of water could be put into the canal for the embankments during this time had remained porous and to have filled the canal to its full depth before the earthen embankments had settled would have caused many more washouts than actually occurred. Beginning in 1840 a four-foot depth of water was finally maintained through the entire canal permitting boats of thirty tons cargo to pass through from Honesdale to Rondout without danger of grounding.

During July, 1841, Washington Irving accompanied Philip Hone, Henry Brevoort and representatives of the Board of Managers on a trip through the canal to Honesdale and over "The Gravity" to the mines. Referring to the trip, Hone says in his diary "Their whole voyage was one of mirth and good cheer. They took pleasure in the very inconveniences of the small canal boat, making their beds on the hard planks, eating in primitive fashion and travelling three miles an hour. Geoffrey Crayon (Irving) enjoyed himself to the top of bent. Apparently it was something wonderful for him to forego his day-time nap." Irving *was* impressed with his trip for, from Honesdale, he wrote his sister in Paris:

> "I do not know when I have made a more gratifying excursion with respect to natural scenery—for many miles the canal is built along the face of perpendicular precipices rising into stupendous cliffs, with overhanging forests, or jutting out into vast promontories, while upon the other side you look down upon the Delaware, roaring and foaming below you, at the foot of an immense wall or embankment which supports the canal. Altogether, it is one of the most daring undertakings I have ever witnessed to carry an artificial river over rocky mountains, and up the most savage and almost impracticable defiles. For upward of ninety miles I went through a constant succession of scenery that would have been famous had it existed in any part of Europe."

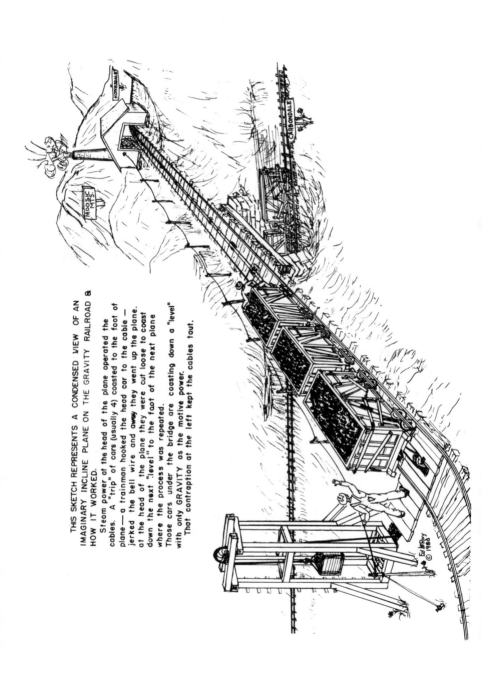

THIS SKETCH REPRESENTS A CONDENSED VIEW OF AN IMAGINARY INCLINE PLANE ON THE GRAVITY RAILROAD & HOW IT WORKED.

Steam power of the head of the plane operated the cables. A "trip" of cars (usually 4) coasted to the foot of plane — a trainman hooked the head car to the cable — jerked the bell wire and away they went up the plane. At the head of the plane they were cut loose to coast down the next "level" to the foot of the next plane where the process was repeated.

Those cars under the bridge are coasting down a "level" with only GRAVITY as the motive power.

That contraption at the left kept the cables taut.

Apparently the excitement of the trip and the exposure was too much for Irving for he was taken ill immediately upon his return home. Hone, however, taking exception to the newspaper accounts, thought the illness due to some other cause.

The business of the company continued to increase during 1841 and 1842 and in September 1842 plans for increasing the capacity of the canal were approved. This enlargement was to be accomplished by raising the heights of and increasing the strength of the embankments sufficiently to maintain a depth of water in the canal of no less than five feet. The material was to be principally taken from the bed of the canal and from the berm bank below the surface of the usual boating head. This enlargement, it was estimated, would permit the use of boats of 40 tons capacity.

Work was actually commenced at the end of the boating season in November, 1842, and continued throughout that winter, but suspended again when the boating season opened in May, 1843, so that the work was not finally completed until the spring of 1844. Because much of the earthwork done on the embankments during the winter just passed, had not settled sufficiently to sustain the full five foot depth without crumbling, the season of 1844 opened with only four feet of water in the canal, but as the boating season progressed the depth was gradually increased as the banks became able to sustain it.

There had sprung up along the line of the canal numerous boat yards owned by private individuals from whom the canal company purchased boats made to their specifications. The forty-ton boats which were now being built to replace the "Flickers," as the first diminutive boats were called, cost the canal company between $360.00 and $375.00 each and were sold to the boatmen for $400.00 to be paid for on the installment plan. The owner of the boat was paid (during 1842) $1.34 per ton for the trip from Honesdale to Rondout but out of this sum $10.00 was retained by the company and credited against the balance owed on the boat. As many of the boats in use in 1842 were still of the "Flicker" class their owners were unable to take advantage in full of the increased capacity of the canal, even though the boats were "hipped" (i.e., their sides raised) to increase their capacity. During the boating season, from early May to early December, a competent boatman could, barring accident, complete fifteen or sixteen trips making it possible for the average boatman to pay for his boat in about three years and, as the average life of a boat was about six years, he was able to operate the boat the remaining three years on his own account.

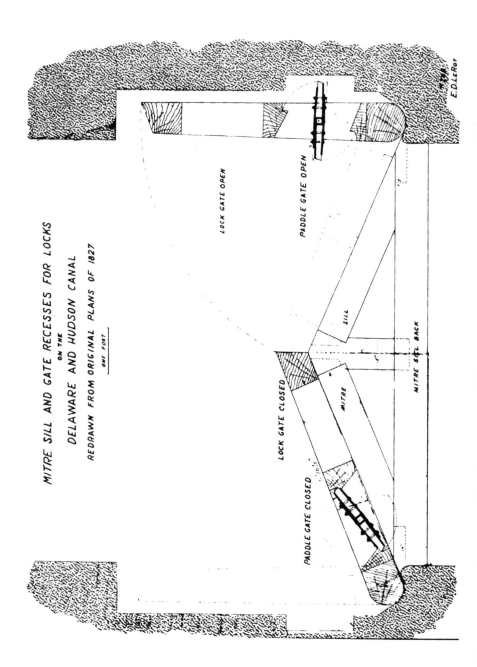

MITRE SILL AND GATE RECESSES FOR LOCKS
ON THE
DELAWARE AND HUDSON CANAL
REDRAWN FROM ORIGINAL PLANS OF 1827
ONE FOOT

LOCK GATE OPEN

PADDLE GATE OPEN

SILL

LOCK GATE CLOSED

MITRE

MITRE SILL BACK

PADDLE GATE CLOSED

E.D.LEROY

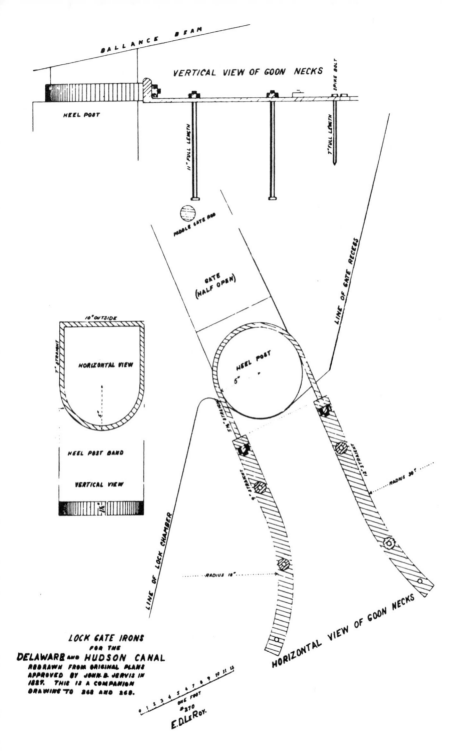

VERTICAL VIEW OF GOON NECKS

BALLANCE BEAM

HEEL POST

11" FULL LENGTH

7" FULL LENGTH

SPIKE BOLT

PADDLE GATE ROD

GATE (HALF OPEN)

LINE OF GATE RECESS

10" OUTSIDE

HORIZONTAL VIEW

7" STRAIGHT

HEEL POST

5"

HEEL POST BAND

VERTICAL VIEW

7¼"

RADIUS 30'

12 STRAIGHT

LINE OF LOCK CHAMBER

RADIUS 18'

HORIZONTAL VIEW OF GOON NECKS

LOCK GATE IRONS
FOR THE
DELAWARE AND HUDSON CANAL
REDRAWN FROM ORIGINAL PLANS
APPROVED BY JOHN B. JERVIS IN
1827. THIS IS A COMPANION
DRAWING TO 268 AND 269.

0 1 2 3 4 5 6 7 8 9 10 11 12
ONE FOOT
#270
E.D.LEROY.

42

THE year 1843 was the first during which the enlarged capacity of the canal was available for the entire season, but even though no less than ninety-seven new boats were put upon the canal that year, there still remained many "Flickers" whose owners were put at a further disadvantage by the reduction in the freight rate to $1.03 per ton for the trip. This reduction affected, in particular, those whose boats were then paid for as in addition the installment deduction was also reduced by the company to $7.00 per trip. True, with their "hipped" boats they could carry greater tonnage than before, but still they grumbled. The canal company, summarizing the substantial saving in cost per ton resulting from the improvements already made upon the canal, decided again to increase the depth to five and one-half feet, which would make possible the use of boats having fifty tons capacity.

Work on this enlargement was begun in 1845 and continued through 1846 but was not completed until the following year, although with this enlargement in prospect about a hundred boats of fifty-ton capacity were built and put into operation during these years. However, until the full head of water could be let into the canal, these boats were not loaded to their full capacity. In fact, even if the enlargement could have been completed by 1845, it is probable that full advantage could not have been taken because of a severe drought which extended over a period of eight weeks that summer, making it impossible to load the boats even to their former capacity. The canal company, to some extent, compensated the boatmen for their loss, by returning the freight rate, which had been cut to 97 cents, to the former rate of $1.03 per ton.

While during 1846 the head of water throughout a large section of the canal had been increased, progress was much slower than had been expected. Even so, it seems that the bed of the canal was now more smooth and as a consequence handling of the boats was easier. Apparently with this in mind the canal company further reduced the freight rate on coal but, as an inducement to the boatmen to make speedier trips, a sliding scale was at this time inaugurated allowing 92 cents per ton on trips of ten days or less which would be equivalent to sixteen trips per season, 88 cents per ton for a trip of eleven days but only 85 cents per ton for trips taking more than eleven days.

During this period, between 1842-45, under the supervision of James Archbald, extensive improvements were made upon the gravity railroad in order to keep pace with the increased capacity of the canal. On the west side of the Moosic Mountains the location of the entire road, with the exception of Plane No. 1 was changed and a better grade, favoring the loaded cars, was obtained. On the east side of the mountain,

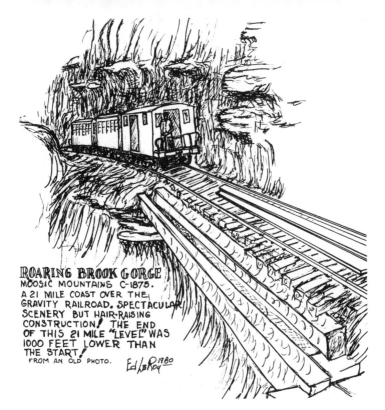

ROARING BROOK GORGE
MOOSIC MOUNTAINS C-1875.
A 21 MILE COAST OVER THE
GRAVITY RAILROAD. SPECTACULAR
SCENERY BUT HAIR-RAISING
CONSTRUCTION! THE END
OF THIS 21 MILE "LEVEL" WAS
1000 FEET LOWER THAN
THE START!
FROM AN OLD PHOTO.  Ed LeRoy 1980

Plane No. 6, which was originally the longest on the road, was divided into two separate planes; also an entirely new and separate track was built from the foot of Plane No. 7 to Honesdale, a distance of ten miles. This was the greatest single improvement, for the original section, between Planes No. 7 and 8, had been single tracked with two-turnouts or sidings. Here the loaded cars now not only had a continuous down grade of ten miles, but it was no longer necessary to lower the loaded cars at Plane No. 8. There were no changes of importance made in the light track east of the summit, but one important improvement was the replacement, throughout the length of the road, of the old wood and strap iron rails by the new "T" iron rails manufactured at Slocum Hollow (Scranton).

In spite of these substantial improvements on the canal and the gravity railroad the demand for anthracite was growing so rapidly that it could not be met. The improvements on the canal had cost the company slightly more than $250,000, but the savings in the cost of transporting the company's own coal had exceeded that figure by 50%, even including the period when the full capacity of the canal was not yet available, but by 1847 the "Flickers" had largely disappeared from the canal, the 40-tonners had themselves been "hipped" and the newest boats were now able to carry as much as 55 tons without danger of grounding. In short, the year 1847 was, in spite of the usual delays from freshets and washouts, a good one, for over seven thousand cargoes of cal were carried

44

NEAR NAPANOCH, NY
LOCK #27

45

to tidewater between April 25, when the canal opened, and December 4th, when it was closed by freezing.

With these facts at hand, the board of managers on November 17th, 1847, approved the recommendations of chief engineer R. F. Lord for the enlargement of the entire canal to a minimum depth of six feet. They included the enlargement of the locks which were to be further improved by the addition of more paddle gates to speed up the passage of boats.

*Extract from a report of R. F. Lord, Esq., dated January 6th, 1847.*

The original plan upon which the canal was constructed afforded 4 feet depth of water, and a maximum capacity for boats carrying cargoes of 30 tons.

The lowest rate of freight for which boatmen had been obtained in the coal business up to the year 1843, was $1.34 per ton ; and it is not probable, that for any considerable increase of business, they could have been retained at that rate ; for at that they were more or less transient, and frequently abandoned their boats.

In the month of September, 1842, a plan was adopted for enlarging the canal, to be accomplished by raising the height and increasing the strength of its banks and appendages, with materials taken mainly from its bed and berm side, below the surface of the usual boating head, sufficient to sustain 5 feet depth of water, improve its channel, and make it competent for boats to navigate it, carrying 40 ton cargoes, with a view of making a more desirable business for boatmen, and thereby reduce the rate of freight.

The improvement was commenced in the fall of 1842, and was prosecuted a considerable extent the ensuing winter, in order to realize in part its benefits for the year 1843, and to have it completed during the season of 1844.

The depth of water was gradually increased during the season of navigation as the banks were prepared to sustain it. Its immediate effects were apparent, from the boats which were adapted to the former head of 4 feet being able to carry an increased cargo, in proportion to the additional depth of water. The best class of these boats had their sides raised in order to improve the offered advantages ; and new boats were built on an enlarged plan, to correspond with the improved canal.

During the years 1845 and 1846 a considerable proportion of the boats were of the old pattern, and adapted only to the first proposed enlargement, being competent to carry only 40 to 45 tons, while the new enlarged boats carried 48 and 50 tons ; consequently the average freight for those two years does not exhibit so clearly the advantages of the improvement as it did for the two years of 1843 and 1844, when the boats were more competent to improve the increased facilities. The old pattern boats are being paid for and their number considerably reduced every season, and their places supplied with boats built to correspond with the enlargement. Nearly all the old pattern boats will be withdrawn from the coal business during the years 1847 and 1848 ; after which the rate of freight can be brought down to correspond with the enlargement and increased facilities of navigation.

In 1842, 30 tons at $1.34 paid the boatmen $40.20 pr.trip
    "  50  "    84 cents will pay them  42.00 "  "

The result of the improvements on the canal will be—

1st. Increased strength and permanent solidity to resist the action of floods.

2d. Additional facilities and certainty of navigation on it.

3d. A large increase of its permanent capacity.

4th. A permanent reduction of about 50 cents per ton on the rate of freight.

All of which has been obtained without interrupting the regular navigation and business of the canal.

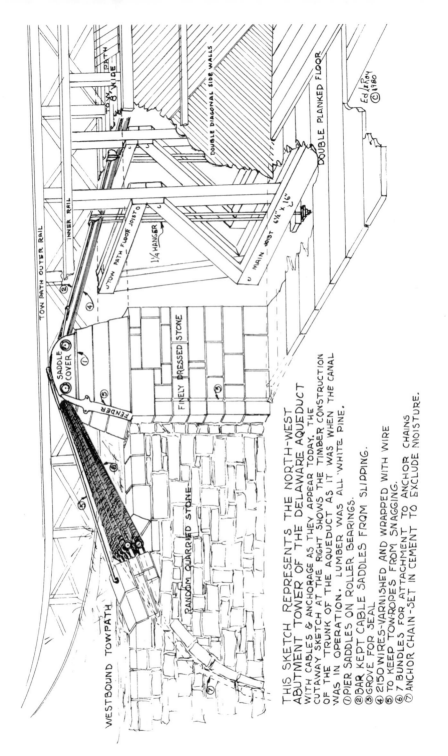

THIS SKETCH REPRESENTS THE NORTH-WEST
ABUTMENT TOWER OF THE DELAWARE AQUEDUCT
WITH CABLES & ANCHORAGE AS THEY APPEAR TODAY. THE
CUTAWAY SKETCH AT THE RIGHT SHOWS THE TIMBER CONSTRUCTION
OF THE TRUNK OF THE AQUEDUCT AS IT WAS WHEN THE CANAL
WAS IN OPERATION. LUMBER WAS ALL WHITE PINE.
① PIER SADDLES ON ROLLER BEARINGS.
② BAR KEPT CABLE SADDLES FROM SLIPPING.
③ GROVE FOR SEAL.
④ 2150 WIRES-VARNISHED AND WRAPPED WITH WIRE
⑤ TO KEEP TOW-ROPES FROM SNAGGING.
⑥ 7 BUNDLES FOR ATTACHMENT TO ANCHOR CHAINS
⑦ ANCHOR CHAIN-SET IN CEMENT TO EXCLUDE MOISTURE.

TOW PATH OUTER RAIL
INNER RAIL
TOW PATH FLOOR JOISTS
¼ HANGER
MAIN JOIST 6½" x 16"
DOUBLE DIAGONAL SIDE WALLS
DOUBLE PLANKED FLOOR
10" WIDE
SADDLE COVER
FENDER
FINELY DRESSED STONE
RANDOM QUARRIED STONE
WESTBOUND TOWPATH

Ed/Roy
©1980

48

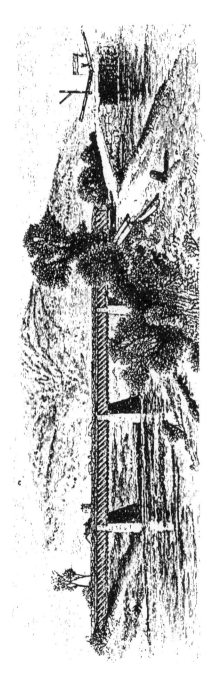

FIGURE 12.—At a time when public works wrought less havoc to the landscape than today, engineering structures could frequently be appreciated for their visual as well as their technical contribution, even in an area as scenically hallowed as the upper Delaware Valley. A contemporary view of the Delaware Aqueduct from William Cullen Bryant's *Picturesque America*, volume 2. COURTESY SMITHSONIAN.

The bank of the canal along the Lackawaxen and Delaware Rivers was to be made more secure against the wash from the boats by the erection of stonework where necessary, for there had been many delays resulting from boats grounding on sandbars caused by the inside embankment washing down into the canal. The work of enlargement was begun upon the cessation of boating early in December, 1847, and about the same time Chief Engineer Lord made a trip to Pittsburgh to examine the aqueduct built by John A. Roebling who many years later was to win everlasting fame as the engineer of the great Brooklyn Bridge. Lord's report was most favorable for the Pittsburgh aqueduct was a substantial work and Roebling s engineering ability was far ahead of the times. Roebling was engaged to begin work for the D. & H. at once.

Construction of these aqueducts, when the company was able to finance them, had been contemplated since 1841. In fact John Wurts stated, at the Kingston hearings in 1858, that they had been under consideration from the very early days of the canal but in any event their construction was hastened by the approach of the Erie Railroad into the Delaware Valley as the D. & H. wished to prevent the prior location of the Erie tracks from affecting the most advantageous location of the new canal route.

*Estimate of Repairs and Superintendence of Canal in 1847.*

| | |
|---|---:|
| Wages of lock-tenders, oil-lamps, &c | $17,000 00 |
| Repairs on lock-tenders' houses, roofs, chimneys, sills, &c | 1,200 00 |
| Repairs on locks, paddle-gates, floors, sluices, &c | 5,000 00 |
| Repairs on waste-weirs, bulkheads, acqueducts, bridges, railing on high slope-walls, &c | 3,500 00 |
| Repairs on feeder-dams, bulwarks, reservoirs, &c | 2,000 00 |
| Winter and spring work, clearing out bed of canal, &c.. | 8,000 00 |
| Five superintendents at $650 each, and one at $750 per annum | 4,000 00 |
| 128 men, including mechanics, watchmen and laborers, at an average of $24 per month, including use of tools, &c., for eight months | 24,576 00 |
| 21 horses, towing gravel scows, &c., at $16 per month, including harness, keeping, &c., eight months | 2,688 00 |
| Salary of engineer $2,500, stationery, postage, &c. $125. | 2,625 00 |
| Add for contingencies | 6,000 00 |
| Total | $76,589 00 |
| Estimated amount of canal tolls in 1847 | 25,000 00 |
| Excess | $51,589 00 |

There will probably be required for the construction of
Delaware Aqueduct, during the year 1847........ $40,000 00
There are 81 canal boats being built on line of canal at
$410 per boat............................. $33,210 00

Roebling completed the masonry on the Delaware aqueduct in January, 1848, at which time the cut stone for the Lackawaxen aqueduct was on hand and Engineer Lord wrote to Mr. Wurts stating that both spans would be ready for use in the fall of 1848. However, they were not brought into use until April 26th, 1849, when the canal opened for the season.

Poling the boats across the Delaware, on the pond created by the dam just below the mouth of the Lackawaxen, had always been slow, dangerous and subject to frequent delays because of high water in the spring and fall. The mules seem to have been the only one to profit by the old route for they were afforded a well-earned rest as they were carried across the old rope ferry.

The new aqueducts necessitated the construction of three new locks (Numbers 70, 71 and 72) on the Delaware to bring the boats to the new high level but at the same time locks Numbers 1, 2 and 3 on the Lackawaxen were eliminated. The Lackawaxen aqueduct crossed that river three hundred yards above its mouth, the Delaware span about the same distance below. There being no physical obstruction to prevent it, why did not the company build a single aqueduct across the Delaware River above the mouth of the Lackawaxen, rather than bridging both rivers?

—Invitation to supply lumber for the Delaware and Lackawaxen aqueducts.
(Courtesy of Rensselaer Polytechnic Institute.)

These aqueducts are monuments to the engineering skill and courage of their builder.

The Delaware span, now (1945) a highway bridge, is probably the oldest suspension span still in use. Roebling built to endure and never did he compromise for economy's sake. He demanded the best material available, the most exacting workmanship and personally supervised every detail.

CABLE ANCHORAGE

In January, 1849, Roebling wrote to Henry V. Poor, in New York, giving the following specifications:

"Delaware aqueduct, four spans, 132 to 142 feet each.

| | |
|---|---|
| Trunk width at bottom | 17 feet 6 inches |
| Trunk width at top | 20 feet |
| Depth of water | 6 feet |
| Weight of water in 142 foot span | 484 tons |
| Tension of cables | 708 tons |
| Diameter of cables | 8½ inches |
| Each cable contains | 2150 wires |
| Cable wt per lineal foot | 130 lbs. |
| Ultimate strength of cables | 3870 tons |

Lackawaxen aqueduct two spans 114 feet each

Each Cable seven inches in diameter

(Same as Pittsburgh aqueduct)

The wires do not extend below the ground but connect with anchor chains, the cross section of which exceeds that of the wire by 50%.

Strength of wire being 90,000 lbs. per superficial inch while chains will not bear over 60,000 lbs."

Later that year, Roebling is quoted in the Honesdale Democrat as stating that there were 7688 cubic yards of hydraulic cement masonry in the Delaware aqueduct.

More modern bridges have been swept away but Roebling's have withstood every flood and ice for almost a century.

While the construction of these aqueducts was in progress, construction was begun on suspension aqueducts to replace the original wood and stone aqueduct across the Neversink River near Cuddebackville and the stone arch aqueduct across Rondout Creek at High Falls. Except that these aqueducts were single spans they were similar in construction to the Delaware and Lackawaxen aqueducts. Both were ready for operation when the 1851 season opened. Speaking of the Delaware and Lackawaxen aqueducts, Chief Engineer Lord estimated that they had avoided delays due to high water totaling nine days during their first year of use and furthermore, with the elimination of the first three Lackawaxen locks, the delay in getting the mules on board the ferry and in putting the boat itself across the Delaware, not less than one day was saved each trip.

During the years in which the aqueducts were under construction, the canal was very active, for the demand for Lackawaxen anthracite was increasing rapidly and every effort was being made to meet it, but nature and the Erie Railroad seemed bound to thwart them. During the season of 1847, which opened March 26, flood waters held up the boats at the Delaware Crossing and at Honesdale for two days in May. In June a breach occurred on the summit level which held up the boats for nine days. In July a freshet made the Delaware impassable for two days and in August a breach occurred at White Mills, blocking traffic for a day and a half. Labor was scarce because of the construction then going forward on the Erie Railroad and elsewhere, and the price of oats, hay, and provisions had risen to new heights. To offset these difficulties, the company offered to pay the boatmen a premium of $2.00 per trip, but this does not seem to have been sufficient inducement, so the freight rate was increased to $1.00, 96 cents, or 92 cents per ton, depending upon the length of the trip. Still, the boat owners were not at all satisfied, for those who were still operating smaller boats, which were not fully paid for, did not bother to care for them and in some instances abandoned them outright.

D.+H. Lock

A T DEPOSIT in the Delaware Valley just north of the Pennsylvania line, on November 7, 1835, ground was broken for the construction of the New York, Lake Erie, and Western Railroad, now the "Erie." It will be recalled that the sponsors of the D. & H. Canal had hoped that a branch canal would eventually be built up the Delaware from the mouth of the Lackawaxen. It never materialized, nor did the Erie reach the Delaware Valley for another twelve years, for, after the elaborate ceremonies at Deposit, there were no funds to proceed with the work.

### Early Survey Discounted

In this connection a map by Daniel Burr, dated 1839, is of interest as it shows the route originally surveyed for the Erie. A more accurate survey in 1845 proved this route to be too mountainous and the attention of the Erie engineers was directed to the Valley of the Delaware which was already occupied by the Delaware & Hudson Canal. Erie engineer A. C. Morton proposed building the railroad along the route of the canal. The route was surveyed and it was found that between Port Jervis and the mouth of the Lackawaxen it would be necessary to bridge the canal seven times but, what is more astounding, he proposed that, under Hawke's Nest Mountain, the railroad should be built upon the bed of the river. The canal already hugged the base of the cliff which rises several hundred feet abruptly out of the river. How long such a roadbed would have withstood the battering of the ice is a moot question.

The canal company (to the good fortune of the Erie) lost no time in obtaining an injunction prohibiting the Erie from building over this route, leaving but one alternative—the Erie must cross over into Pike County. The difficulties of obtaining the necessary legislation both from Pennsylvania and New York State are not pertinent to this story, but when the citizens of Wayne County learned that the Erie was about to come into their State a number of them seeing the benefit to be derived from it, made strenuous efforts to induce the Erie to consider a route up the Lackawaxen, past Honesdale, to the headwaters of Starucca Creek and thence to the Susquehanna River, but they were stalemated at every turn for the then existent legislature would not permit the use of this route and at each meeting called by these far-seeing citizens, every proposal favoring the Erie was voted down. It developed later that the canal company had "packed" the meeting with its employes and their friends. This route, by the way, was some twenty miles shorter and of much easier grade than the one followed.

### Reasons for Obstructions

The Delaware & Hudson Canal Company, it now appears, had two reasons for obstructing these plans: first, they feared the Erie as a rival coal carrier, and second, they were then in the process of buying more coal lands in the Lackawanna Valley and the approach of the Erie most certainly would have caused the value of these lands to sky-rocket. (At the time, Senator Dimmick, of Honesdale, represented Wayne and Pike

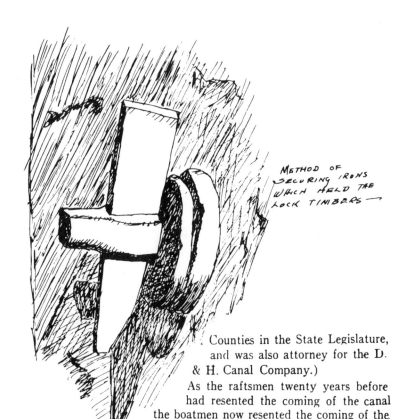

METHOD OF
SECURING IRONS
WHICH HELD THE
LOCK TIMBERS →

Counties in the State Legislature, and was also attorney for the D. & H. Canal Company.)

As the raftsmen twenty years before had resented the coming of the canal the boatmen now resented the coming of the. Railroad, through the valley of the Delaware, for they. saw in it a threat to their means of livelihood, but again it is hard to say which side was the aggressor. The intruding railroad crossed the line of the canal at what now is the town of Lackawaxen, but at the time the Erie was under construction through Pike County, the railroad bridge across the Delaware at Saw Mill Rift had not yet been completed. Consequently, when a locomotive was needed to speed the construction in the Delaware section, the new engine "Piermont" was dismantled and shipped through the canal to Lackawaxen. The shriek of the "Piermont's" whistle terrorized the canal mules and heaped coals on the fire, but this was of minor importance compared to the havoc caused by the blasting being done between Saw Mill Rift and Shohola. Here the hard feeling between the boatmen and the railroad builders flared into open conflict.

### "Wild Irish" Labor

The Erie (as had the D. & H. before them) used newly imported "wild Irish" laborers who would rather fight than eat. It was alleged by the boatmen that the blasts were set off by the workmen only as a boat was passing and that as a result stones, roots of trees, and clods of earth were hurled across the river onto the passing boats.

The Erie side stepped the issue by denying that they had any control over the contractors and the D. & H. made several fruitless attempts to obtain injunctions against the contractors but the danger continued, in fact it grew worse and according to one account "violent personal attacks were made upon boatmen by laborers in which severe injuries were sustained by some of the boatmen." The situation became so serious that the women and children could no longer be taken on the boats and many of the men themselves refused to operate boats between Port Jervis and Lackawaxen. On June 3, 1848, a large party of railroad laborers waylaid a number of boatmen near Mongaup and in the fight which followed severe injuries were sustained by both sides. Some of the leaders were caught and imprisoned but the menace continued so long as the workmen were in that section of the valley and throughout most of the season of 1848 many boats lay abandoned while their captains and crews sought work elsewhere.

### Larger Boats Built

In the meantime the work of enlargement was progressing as well as could be expected in view of the difficulties and throughout the length of the canal many boat builders were busy building larger boats to meet the growing demand. One of the first of these large boats to be built for the D. & H. Company was built by William Turner at Honesdale. Finished in October, 1848, it was launched in the spring of 1849, and, being 91 feet in length, 14½ feet wide, and 8 feet high, it was much too large for the canal at that time, so it was floated down the Lackawaxen and Delaware Rivers to Trenton, thence through the Delaware and Raritan Canal to New York Bay and up the Hudson to Rondout. (Those Lacka-

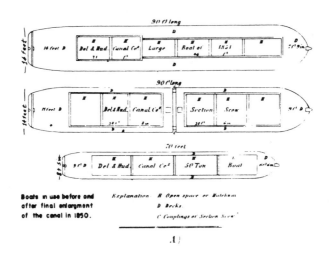

Boats in use before and after final enlargement of the canal in 1850.

waxen raftsmen would try anything once.) Turner himself acted as captain.

Towards the close of the season of 1848, and in 1849, traffic on the canal was again on the increase and the locks throughout the canal were ordered to be kept open eighteen hours a day, from four a. m. to ten p. m. Some locks where traffic jams were most likely to occur, because of the short levels between them, were to be kept open all night. These were Neversink locks 55 to 60 and Lackawaxen locks 1 to 6. In addition, Creek Locks were given extra help.

## Labor Troubles

One difficulty after another seems to have beset the company, and now with laborers still in demand, the boatmen continued their independent

*Rowland's, The D.&H. Canal*

attitude and to grumble at every possible delay. Now, they complained, the loading facilities at Honesdale were inadequate, and caused many delays; consequently the company wisely continued the inducements previously offered but when, on June 25, 1849, cholera broke out at Rondout, the boatmen became alarmed and, when the plague spread along the line of the canal, hundreds of boatmen, lock tenders and other workers forsook the canal for work in far-away places where they would not be exposed to the dread plague. In fact, so many left their jobs on the canal that season that normal operations could not be resumed until the following year.

In the twenty years during which the Delaware and Hudson Canal had been in operation, the public had gradually come to realize that anthracite coal was far more practicable as a fuel than wood. All of the facilities of the company combined were not now sufficient to supply the demands of the expanding market so, when the Washington Coal Company, with coal lands in the lower Lackawanna Valley was organized, in 1847, the board of managers of the D. & H. at once realized that the business of this rival could be turned into an asset if the D. & H. could handle the transportation of their coal. Accordingly, an open letter addressed to the citizens of Luzern County was published in local papers. In it were set forth the "favorable tolls on articles reaching the D. & H. Canal by means of a railroad to be constructed through Cobbs Gap." There was, however, a joker in the offer, for the toll on coal was to be governed by the price brought by D. & H. coal at Rondout. At the same time, consideration was given to the possibility of extending the D. & H. Company's gravity railroad to a junction with that of the Washington Coal Company at Providence, but this move was decided against, for the capacity of the "Gravity," even with its recent improvements, would not be equal to half that of the enlarged canal. In August, 1847, an agreement between the D. & H. and the Washington Coal Company was arrived at, but this agreement was still based upon the D. & H. Company's selling price at Rondout, for it provided that "$2.50 shall be deducted from price coal brings at Rondout and one-half of the remainder shall be the toll per ton for that calendar year". BUT it also provided that "In case of an enlargement of the canal, the company (the D. & H.) may charge the toll at a rate per ton to be established after the enlargement is completed, to be based upon an estimate of reduction of cost of transportation produced by the enlargement."

OFFICE OF THE DELAWARE AND HUDSON CANAL CO., }
New York, April 24th, 1847. }

The Board met.

Present—The PRESIDENT.

Messrs. Herriman,        Talbot,
    "    Hawley,          Le Roy,
    "    Young,           Post,
    "    Holmes,          Platt, Vice-President.

\*      \*      \*      \*      \*      \*      \*      \*

A report, of which the following is a copy, was presented by the committee to whom was referred the communication of the president to the board at the meeting of the 23d December last :

The committee to whom was referred the devising of a plan to fill up the capacity of the canal, in order to an increase of the revenue of the company, have reflected much upon the subject, and it is with regret they are compelled to state their embarrassment in recommending a plan likely to accomplish so desirable an end.

If a railroad could be made from the lower part of the Lackawanna Valley to connect with the canal, said road to be in a measure under the control of the Delaware and Hudson Canal Company, and the coal brought thereby so disposed of at Rondout as not to conflict with the sales and general business of the company, the committee would feel little loss in recommending a tariff of tolls which might induce capitalists and owners of coal-lands (if they can be so induced) to make a road; but, as the opinion has been expressed by persons supposed to be more familiar than your committee with the feelings of the residents in the lower part of the Valley, that a road, if made, must be a public one, free to all who desire to have coal transported thereon, with, of course, a like freedom on the canal and sales of coal at Rondout, the committee feel embarrassed as to the measures which may be most wise for the board to adopt. Under these embarrassments, in view of the decided expression of the president heretofore made of the propriety of a tariff of tolls, the committee suggest that it may be wise in the board to make a tariff of tolls, and that the same be fixed at one-fifth of the sum at which the Delaware and Hudson Canal Company shall sell their coal at Rondout. This rate not to be increased prior to the year (1860) eighteen hundred and sixty, unless the company shall expend money to double or enlarge the locks, or otherwise improve the canal, by which enlargement or improvement freight on coal shall be reduced; in such case, said reduction shall accrue to the company by increase of tolls over rates above named.

Which is respectfully submitted.

New York, April 13th, 1847.

W. M. HALSTED.
ISAAC L. PLATT.
IRAD HAWLEY.
SILAS HOLMES.
A. G. STOUT.

By an arrangement between the two companies it is stipulated, that the coal entering the canal from the new road shall pay to this company a canal toll equal to half the difference between $2 50 and the market price of coal at Rondout, which market price shall be determined in each and every year by ascertaining the average rate per ton of the sales of the Del. and Hudson Canal Co., up to the first of May, and if the canal shall be enlarged, this toll is to be increased, by adding thereto half the amount thereby saved in freight, as compared with the rate of freight paid on the present canal. This arrangement must add largely to the revenue of the Delaware and Hudson Canal Company, and, taken in connection with the considerations which have already been submitted, presents, in the opinion of the Board, conclusive reasons for an enlargement of the canal.

If, for example, the market price of the coal at Rondout should be four dollars per ton, the toll to be paid by the new company to the Del. and Hud. Canal Co., irrespective of any enlargement of the canal, would be 75 cents a ton, and if, by the enlargement of the canal, a saving of 40 cents per ton be made in freight, it would make the toll 95 cents. This, on a business of 500,-000 tons from the new road, would yield to the Del. and Hud. Canal Co., the sum of 475,000 dollars, and if to that be added the assumed saving that this company would make on its own quantity of 500,000 tons, viz., 40 cents a ton, the aggregate gain to the company would be 675,000 dollars. This sum will be considerably increased by a large amount of miscellaneous trade that will be drawn to the canal by the new railroad. It will penetrate the valley of both the Lackawanna and Susquehannah rivers, reach the public improvements of Pennsylvania, and open a country rich in resources, whose trade has hitherto taken a different route, but the natural channel for which will be the Delaware and Hudson Canal as soon as the new road is finished. It would be difficult, and perhaps unsatisfactory, to attempt an estimate of the revenue likely to be derived from this source. But it could not fail to carry the aggregate considerably beyond 700,000 dollars.

When we read this agreement we cannot but wonder whether or not the Washington Company signed "with their tongue in their cheeks" but as has been pointed out that while the charter of the Delaware & Hudson Company limited the toll charged on general commodities, the toll on coal was not so limited; hence they were within their rights in this agreement. Work on this new railroad, which was to be a gravity road, closely patterned after the D. & H. Gravity, was begun on March 28, 1848, and shortly thereafter the Washington Coal Company merged with the Pennsylvania Coal Company, assuming the name of the latter.

Among the names of the founders of the Washington Coal Company is that of John Wurts, who was then president of the Delaware & Hudson Canal Company, but he seems to have dropped out shortly after the consolidation of the Washington and Pennsylvania Coal Companys. Irad Hawley, a New York City engineer and financier, was elected president of the new Pennsylvania Coal Company and it is only fitting that, as the building of this company's railroad contributed so greatly to the growth of the town, which mushroomed overnight from a raftsmen's village of a few houses into a booming town, should be named "Hawleysburg" in his honor.

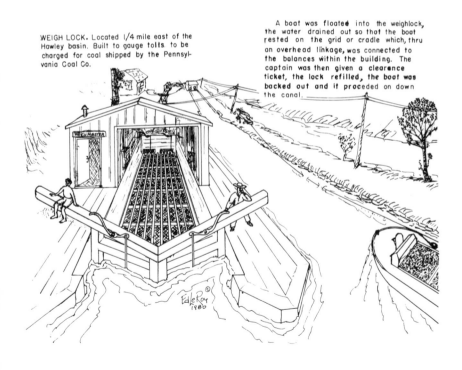

WEIGH LOCK. Located 1/4 mile east of the Hawley basin. Built to gauge tolls. to be charged for coal shipped by the Pennsylvania Coal Co.

A boat was floated into the weighlock, the water drained out so that the boat rested on the grid or cradle which, thru an overhead linkage, was connected to the balances within the building. The captain was then given a clearance ticket, the lock refilled, the boat was backed out and it proceded on down the canal.

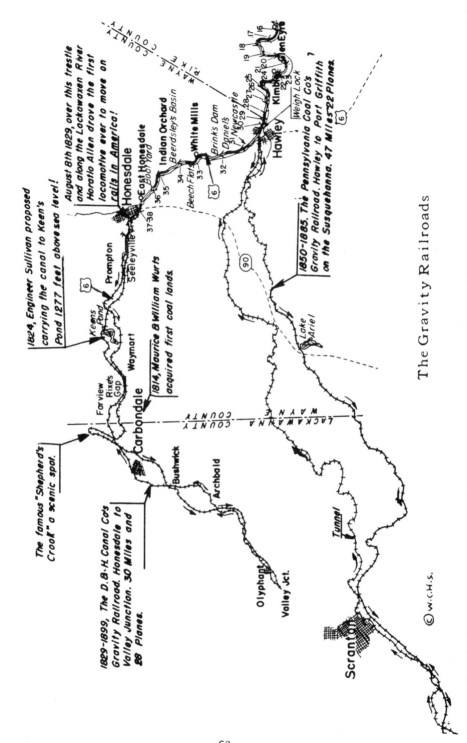

The Gravity Railroads

1824, Engineer Sullivan proposed carrying the canal to Keen's Pond 1277 feet above sea level!

August 8th 1829, over this trestle and along the Lackawaxen River Horatio Allen drove the first locomotive ever to move on rails in America!

WAYNE COUNTY · PIKE COUNTY

Honesdale
Prompton
Seeleyville
Keens Pond
Waymart
Farview
Rixes Gap
Carbondale
Bushwick
Archbald
Olyphant
Valley Jct.
Scranton
Tunnel

East Honesdale
Bootyard
Indian Orchard
Beerdsleys Basin
Beech Flats
White Mills
Brink's Dam
Daniels
Newcastle
Hawley
Kimble
Glen Eyre
Weigh Lock
Lake Ariel

LACKAWANNA COUNTY
WAYNE COUNTY

37-38
36
35
34
33
32
31
30 29
28 27 26 25
24 20
21
22
23
19 18
17
16

6

90

1814, Maurice & William Wurts acquired first coal lands

The famous "Shepherd's Crook" a scenic spot.

1829-1899, The D.&H. Canal Co's Gravity Railroad. Honesdale to Valley Junction. 30 Miles and 28 Planes.

1850-1865, The Pennsylvania Coal Co's Gravity Railroad. Hawley to Port Griffith on the Susquehanna. 47 Miles, 22 Planes.

© W.C.H.S.

63

## Telegraph on the Canal

Another important innovation which was introduced along the canal during these fast-moving years was the telegraph, for in 1848 the canal company granted permission to an organization, out of which developed the Western Union Telegraph Company, to construct a telegraph line along its right of way. The line ran from Lake Erie following the turnpike through Owego, Montrose and Dundaff to Carbondale; thence along the right of way of the "Gravity" to Honesdale, then down along the canal tow path to Port Jervis, from which place it followed the newly completed Erie Railroad to the Hudson River.

The next year, 1849, the Erie Railroad, or to use the full name by which it was then known, The New York, Lake Erie and Western, had completed the laying of its track through the Delaware Valley, but in spite of the rivalry and ill will which then existed between them, the D. & H. constructed a canal basin at the present town of Lackawaxen for the transfer of freight between the rivals. The Erie was, however, not yet a serious competitor.

## Boat Yard at Hawley

Also in 1849 Levi Barker, anticipating the demand for many more boats to haul the coal of the Pennsylvania Coal Company, left the employ of Christopher Lane's boat works at Honesdale and established a boatyard and drydock at Hawley. He was immediately given a contract by the Pennsylvania Company for the construction of twenty-five deck-type boats which were to have a capacity of one hundred forty tons in anticipation of the enlargement of the canal. These were somewhat larger in capacity than those being built for the D. & H., but were as fine as any boat ever put upon the canal and cost $1,600 each. Barker, during the forty years he continued in business at Hawley, built over six hundred boats.

Although many hundred Irish and German laborers were brought into the country, at the time the Pennsylvania Company's Gravity road was being built, the D. & H. Company required many laborers for the work of enlargement of the canal and the Erie needed hundreds more, nevertheless, work on the Pennsylvania Gravity progressed fairly well. This newcomer was able to profit greatly by the experience of twenty years of operation of the D. & H. Gravity line, and furthermore, iron (but not steel) rails were being conveniently manufactured by the Scranton brothers at Slocum Hollow. Thus they could avoid one great handicap which had retarded the D. & H. The road was patterned closely after the D. & H. but was much longer; forty-seven miles to the seventeen of the early D. & H. Both the loaded track and the light track were the same length but followed widely separated routes. They were, in fact, five miles apart at one point. Much better use than in the building of the D. & H. Gravity was made of the contour of the country through which it ran, for on the loaded track one of the "levels" measured fourteen miles, while one on the light track measured twenty-one. On the loaded track there were twelve ascending planes and ten descending "levels" but on the light track there were ten ascending planes and twelve descending "levels."

## Operation of Planes

All of the motive power on the loaded track was furnished by stationary steam engines at the head of each plane but on the light track the first four planes counting west from Hawley were operated by water power obtained from Middle Creek.

Coal breakers, repair shops, storage yards, and a canal basin were built at Hawley and for a few years that little town went through an era of prosperity matched only by the gold rush towns of the same year. Their railroad was finished and the Pennsylvania Coal Company was able to begin shipping coal from Hawley on June 8, 1850, but although the enlargement of the canal was almost entirely completed, it was not possible to load the new boats with more than one hundred tons each.

SECTIONAL VIEW - DELAWARE AQUEDUCT
DELAWARE & HUDSON CANAL. WITH LOADED
(EASTBOUND) BOAT. THE RESISTANCE TO A LOADED BOAT PASSING
THRU THIS NAROW FLUME MUST HAVE BEEN CONSIDERABLE!

THE AQUEDUCT WAS 17' WIDE AT BOTTOM &
20' WIDE AT TOP. DEPTH OF WATER 6 FT.
THE 140 TON BOATS WERE 14' WIDE & WHEN
LOADED HAD A DRAUGHT OF 5'.

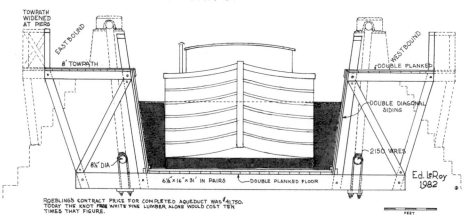

TOWPATH WIDENED AT PIERS
EASTBOUND
8' TOWPATH
8½' DIA
6½"×16"×31' IN PAIRS
DOUBLE PLANKED FLOOR
WESTBOUND
DOUBLE PLANKED
DOUBLE DIAGONAL SIDING
2150 WIRES
Ed. LeRoy 1982
FEET

ROEBLINGS CONTRACT PRICE FOR COMPLETED AQUEDUCT WAS $41,750.
TODAY THE KNOT FREE WHITE PINE LUMBER ALONE WOULD COST TEN
TIMES THAT FIGURE.

This last enlargement of the canal had been more an enlargement of the locks rather than the trunk of the canal itself, for while this latter was made navigable for one hundred forty-ton boats, this was accomplished by changing the prism of the canal by cutting out the lower portion of the sloping sides of the canal and building these up, nearly vertical, with dry stone walls. Thus while the canal was deepened and made navigable for boats of greatly increased capacity, the surface width was increased only slightly throughout most of the length of the canal. It should be remembered that, as originally constructed, the canal measured thirty-two feet in width at the water line, but only twenty feet wide at the bottom. The original boats had a maximum width of only eight feet, four inches, whereas the large boats had a width of fourteen feet, four inches; therefore, a cross section of the canal was now only three times that of a loaded large boat, whereas in the old canal it had been at least four-and-a-half times that of the smaller boats. The result was greater resistance to be overcome in proportion to the size of the boats used.

As was to be expected, the embankments had not, during the first two years after the enlargement, become sufficiently water-tight to hold the full six-foot head of water. As a result, the large boats could be loaded only to about two-thirds of their capacity, but nevertheless, they were much slower than the many smaller old boats which were still in use. Consequently, they caused considerable annoyance to the masters of the small boats who, in spite of the rules for navigating the canal, were not "afforded reasonable facility to pass by" although the penalty for each violation of this rule was ten dollars. Until the small boats, the forty and fifty tonners, were finally gone from the canal, the infraction of this one rule probably caused more fights between crews than any other one cause on this, the most business-like of all canals.

## Enlargement Problems

The greatest amount of labor in this enlargement was expended on the locks, which had to be rebuilt throughout. The new locks were one hundred feet in length and fifteen feet wide, except the six near Summitville, which were slightly wider. The original locks had been seventy-six feet in length by nine feet wide.

The increase in the size of these locks presented a problem in itself, for while the capacity of the smaller locks had averaged six thousand, eight hundred cubic feet; consequently, the loss of water each time a boat locked through was much greater. To supply this new need, in case of drought, several new reservoirs were built and the existing feeder dams were raised and improved.

The location of all of the locks remained the same, except for locks 1, 2 and 3, near the mouth of the Lackawaxen River, which had been eliminated by the construction of the two aqueducts there.

Upon the completion of this enlargement the D. & H. Company decided to experiment with different type boats and accordingly purchased forty square-bowed section scows from the Lehigh Canal. It appears that the company did not depart from this practice of "Hiring out" these boats and accordingly contracted for their operation through two men, Barnes and Harlan. After a brief period of use, these scows, with their square bows, were found to offer too much resistance to the water so a more streamlined (if that word can be applied to a canal boat) bow section was built to match the stern sections with more satisfactory results. Although these section boats or "squeezers" which were really two boats hinged together, do not seem to have met with much favor on the D. & H. Canal, apparently ten more were purchased later in the season of 1850 and to these were added new round nose bow sections, making in all one hundred of these section scows now in use.

LATE at night on the 25th of April, 1851, a terrible fire broke out in the village of Honesdale, and before the flames had been brought under control, almost the whole of the town had been destroyed. The fire is believed to have started in Murray's store on Front Street (Main Street) from where it spread rapidly to the adjoining canal docks, and coal storage yards. The company's loading equipment and many boats in the basin including the old packet boats "Fashion" and "Daniel Webster" were destroyed. Ten days later, by a strange coincidence, Philip Hone, for whom this village had been named, died at the age of seventy-one. He had been the company's greatest benefactor and his influence in political as well as financial circles helped the Delaware and Hudson Canal Company to weather the first difficult years.

An act of the Pennsylvania Legislature, the following year, tended to offset these losses, for it extended the charter privilegs in perpetuity. It will be recalled that the charter granted Maurice Wurts provided that the privileges would revert to the State at the end of thirty years. This would have occurred in 1853.

Although the enlargement had been completed for some time it was not until July 28, 1853, that the full six-foot head of water could finally be let into the canal and the boats loaded to their intended capacity, but a survey made at the time revealed that there were still two hundred forty-seven one-horse, fifty-ton boats still operating on the canal, though they had been "hipped," increasing their capacity to about seventy-five tons. In addition, there were the one hundred remodeled section scows, six hundred thirty-eight of the new large boats, and seventeen "lattice-type" boats with which the D. & H. was experimenting. This latter type boat never proved very satisfactory and, although a few more were added to the fleet during 1854, their number never did exceed twenty-five. This list brings the total number of boats in operation for the D. & H. to just over one thousand, in addition to which there were, by the end of that year, four hundred ninety-five large boats operating for the Pennsylvania Coal Company.

To facilitate handling the increasing volume of coal being shipped by the Pennsylvania Coal Company (3,978 cargoes in 1854) a weigh-lock and collector's office was established at Hawley.

With the acquisition of the business of the Pennsylvania Coal Company in 1850, the income on tolls from sources other than D. & H. coal began a sudden increase reaching a peak in 1864, but, except for approximately $50,000 annual toll from lumber, cement and general merchandise, these tolls were mostly on paper for, owing to the dispute which arose with the Pennsylvania Coal Company over the increase in toll following the enlargement of the canal, these tolls remained for the most part uncollected.

Maurice Wurts, "Father of the D. & H. Canal," died on December 29, 1854. This man, whose foresight and courage had been largely responsible for the development of this great enterprise had lived to see his first meager scratching at the coal outcropping grow into extensive mining operations and his first efforts to float a few raft loads of coal to Philadelphia grow into one of this country's great transportation lines.

SNUBBING POST.

GRANITE DEEPLY
GROOVED BY THE
ROPES.

A new practical, time-saving innovation, the drop-gate, was first tried out on the D. & H. Canal in 1855. This device proved so satisfactory that, as soon as the canal closed for the season, in December of that year, the work of replacing the upper gates of each lock throughout the canal was begun. The work progressed rapidly and by May, 1856, the new gates were ready for use. These new gates, together with the improved machinery for operating the lower gates, which were not in themselves changed, now made it possible for one lock tender to lock a boat through more efficiently and easily than two men had done before.

At this time the practice of basing the freight payment, to the boat owners, upon the length of time taken for the trip was abandoned and the freight rate at ninety-two cents per ton for the trip, with an additional allowance of five cents per ton to boatmasters who conformed strictly with their contract, and the rules for navigating the canal. This rate was not deemed satisfactory by the boatmen, who struck at Eddyville on May 15th, demanding a rate which would enable them to meet the higher living costs. The demands seem to have been justified, for the company's offer of $1.05 per ton was accepted and eight days after the strike had begun, the boats were moving again.

While, during 1855 and again during 1856, over a million tons of coal were hauled through the canal. About half of this quantity was coal of the Pennsylvania Coal Company; still the capacity of the D. & H. Gravity was below that of the canal, but in 1856, even though the coal on hand at tidewater and the capacity of the canal seemed equal to any

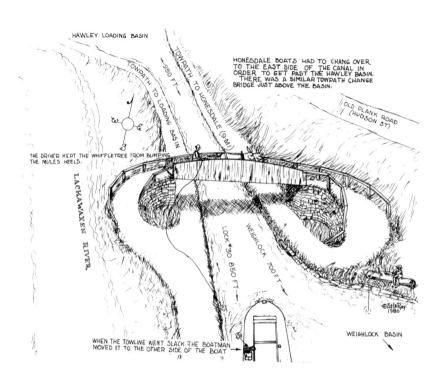

HAWLEY LOADING BASIN

HONESDALE BOATS HAD TO CHANG OVER TO THE EAST SIDE OF THE CANAL IN ORDER TO GET PAST THE HAWLEY BASIN. THERE WAS A SIMILAR TOWPATH CHANGE BRIDGE JUST ABOVE THE BASIN.

TOWPATH TO LOADING BASIN — 950 FT —

TOWPATH TO HONESDALE (9 M.)

OLD PLANK ROAD (HUDSON ST)

THE DRIVER KEPT THE WHIFFLETREE FROM BUMPING THE MULES HEELS.

LACKAWAXEN RIVER

LOCK #30 850 FT

WEIGHLOCK 700 FT

©Ed La Roy 1980

WEIGHLOCK BASIN

WHEN THE TOWLINE WENT SLACK THE BOATMAN MOVED IT TO THE OTHER SIDE OF THE BOAT

demand then in immediate prospect, the board of managers decided to further improve the gravity railroad and enlarge its capacity. The work was begun early in 1856, and continued over a period of two years. This improvement consisted of the relocation of the planes to the west of Rixe's Gap, and the addition of two more planes up the mountain from Carbondale. All of these planes and the intervening levels were double tracked and the grades again improved.

During these two years, the company's business was good and a dividend of eighteen per cent per share was declared in 1855, sixteen per cent in 1856. Eighteen fifty-seven was a depression year, however, and business fell off sharply. In 1858, it reached bottom. Not only did the business of the Canal Company decline sharply, but the Pennsylvania Coal Company had defaulted in the payment of tolls, based upon the previously mentioned contract, to the extent of over six hundred thousand dollars. The dispute over the legality and interpretation of the contract was taken before the courts in 1856, and dragged along for seven years until a verdict in favor of the D. & H. in the amount of three hundred and fifty thousand dollars was finally handed down. True, this was a legal victory for the canal company, but a hollow one, for the sum recovered was less than one-quarter the amount then accrued and, while this legal decision was probably not the only factor involved, it undoubtedly hastened the day when the D. & H. Canal would lose the business of the Pennsylvania Coal Company to the Erie Railroad.

OFFICE OF THE DEL. & HUD. CANAL Co., }
New York, July 28, 1853. }

JOHN EWEN, Esq.,
Prest. of the Penna. Coal Co. :

Dear Sir,—I am instructed by the Board of Managers of this Company to notify the Penna. Coal Co. that the enlargement of the canal of the Delaware and Hudson Canal Co., contemplated by the articles of agreement between it and the Wyoming Coal Association is now completed, and that this Company will hereafter charge and collect the additional toll on coal entering the canal at Hawley, to which it is entitled by said contract.

And I have it further in charge to say, that said Canal Company have, according to the requirement of said agreement, made a fair estimate of the amount of savings in the transportation of coal growing out of said enlargement, and find it to be forty-cents per ton; and said Canal Company therefore claim of said Coal Company the one-half of said amount, that is to say, twenty cents per ton additional toll on all coal hereafter to be transported by said Coal Company on said canal.

Nothing herein contained is intended to waive any claim made by this Company in former communications.

Respectfully,

WM. MUSGRAVE,
V. P.

———

OFFICE OF THE PENNA. COAL Co., }
New York, Augt. 1st, 1853. }

WM. MUSGRAVE, Esq.,
Vice-Prest. Del. & Hud. Canal Co. :

Dear Sir,—Your letter of the 28th ult., in reference to the enlargement of the Delaware and Hudson Canal, and the additional toll to grow out of the same, has been duly received and laid before the Board of Directors of this Company.

I am desired by the Board to inform you that this Company has also made a careful examination in regard to such additional toll, and does not find the savings in the transportation of coal which are alleged in your communication to have been produced by the said enlargement; and that, not being able to agree with your Company in respect thereto, it is ready to proceed in the manner contemplated in such contingency by submitting the matter in difference to the arbitration provided for in the contract to which you have referred.

Respectfully,

John Ewen,<br>Prest.

To place its business on a more independent basis and avoid further friction with the D. & H. over these tolls the Pennsylvania Coal Company in 1860 began the construction of a six-foot gauge steam railroad from Hawley to a junction with the Erie Railroad at Lackawaxen, sixteen miles to the east. While the grade here is about seventeen feet to the mile a continuation of the gravity road was out of the question because the Lackawaxen Valley is very narrow and confined between steep mountain sides. The work progressed slowly and the road was not finished until December 14, 1863, when the first coal train was run over the line. The fact that a railroad could be operated the year round was thus driven home with such emphasis that it could not well be ignored by the managers of the D. & H. Canal and it unquestionably started them thinking in terms of locomotive railroads. In fact, it was the handwriting on the wall insofar as the canal was concerned, although the D. & H. Canal still had many more years of hearty life before it ultimately succumbed in the unequal struggle.

The abrupt change in the outlook of the D. & H. management in favor of railroads is more apparent after reading a letter written by S. B. Ruggles on August 26, 1859, who, while his interest was the Erie Canal and the efforts of railway interests to cripple it, said:

"The Delaware & Hudson Canal now carries 1,300.000 tons of coal in addition to considerable other merchandise and its intelligent officers declare that notwithstanding that their canal is navigable only seven months a year, nothing could induce them to exchange for a railroad."

Within a few years the metamorphosis of the Delaware & Hudson Canal Company into a railroad company was begun; not, however, with any thought in mind of ever abandoning the canal, for the majority of the board of managers remained canal minded for many years. In evidence of this it can be pointed out that in 1869 a substantial majority recommended greatly increasing the capacity of the canal by building double or twin locks, although this enlargement progressed no further than a

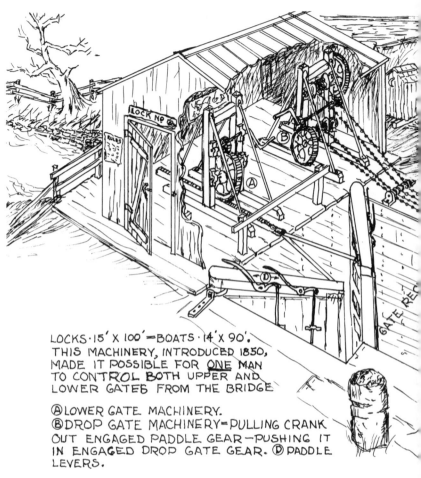

LOCKS·15' X 100'=BOATS·14'X 90'.
THIS MACHINERY, INTRODUCED 1850,
MADE IT POSSIBLE FOR ONE MAN
TO CONTROL BOTH UPPER AND
LOWER GATES FROM THE BRIDGE

Ⓐ LOWER GATE MACHINERY.
Ⓑ DROP GATE MACHINERY=PULLING CRANK
OUT ENGAGED PADDLE GEAR—PUSHING IT
IN ENGAGED DROP GATE GEAR. Ⓓ PADDLE
LEVERS.

WHERE LOCKS WERE CLOSE TOGETHER A CONTRAC
WOULD HIRE OTHER MEN TO OPERATE THEM.

THIS SKETCH IS NOT TO SCALE & SOME ILIBERTY HAS
BEEN TAKEN WITH RELATIVE PROPORTIONS

Ⓔ CUTAWAY TO SHOW DRY STONE WALL-6'THICK TO WH
TIMBER

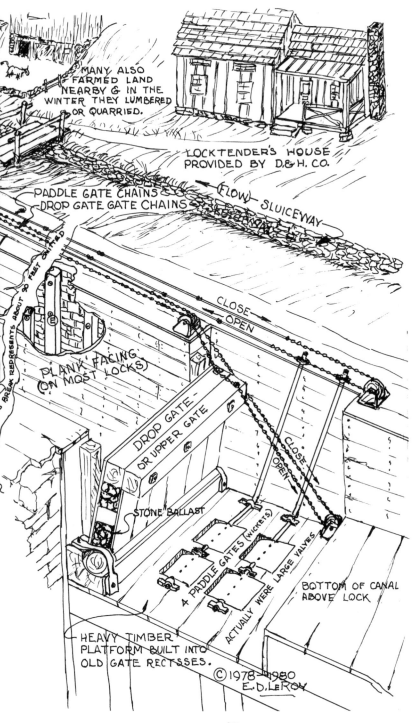

MANY ALSO FARMED LAND NEARBY & IN THE WINTER THEY LUMBERED OR QUARRIED.

LOCKTENDER'S HOUSE PROVIDED BY D.&H. CO.

PADDLE GATE CHAINS
DROP GATE GATE CHAINS

(FLOW) SLUICEWAY

BREAK REPRESENTS ABOUT 90 FEET OMITTED

CLOSE
OPEN

PLANK FACING (ON MOST LOCKS)

DROP GATE - OR UPPER GATE

CLOSE
OPEN

STONE BALLAST

4 PADDLE GATES (WICKETS)

ACTUALLY WERE LARGE VALVES

BOTTOM OF CANAL ABOVE LOCK

HEAVY TIMBER PLATFORM BUILT INTO OLD GATE RECESSES.

©1978–1980
E.D. LeROY

73

pair of terminal locks at Honesdale.

The Pennsylvania Coal Company continued to ship large quantities of coal through the canal from Hawley throughout 1864, but from that year on their shipments decreased almost to the vanishing point, except for the fulfillment of a few of their contracts, along the canal, which could not be reached by the Erie. The Erie had taken over the franchise for the dormant Hudson and Delaware Railroad, mentioned earlier in this story, and had built a branch line to the Hudson River at Newburgh. Consequently, when in 1865 the Pennsylvania Coal Company began shipping the coal via the Erie they moved their storage yards from Port Ewen to Newburgh. Their towboat "Pittston" which had been hauling their boats from tidewater lock at Eddyville to Port Ewen since 1852 was sold to Thomas Cornell, who placed it in service hauling the D. & H. boats to various points on the Hudson River. The tow boat "Maurice Wurts" owned by the canal company, had been placed in service in 1857 and continued its run, hauling boats between Eddyville and Rondout until 1875 when it was replaced by the "Pittston."

Going back a few years in 1851 we find that the Pennsylvania Legislature had just chartered the "Jefferson Railroad" which was proposed to be built over the Lackawaxen route earlier considered by the Erie. Finding the local political opposition of the Delaware & Hudson Canal Company too strong to overcome directly, Charles S. Miner, an attorney of Honesdale, aided by a number of influential citizens, struck upon the simple subterfuge of using the name "Jefferson Railroad." There being no locality in the vicinity having a similar name, they reasoned, the antagonists would not recognize the bill before the Legislature. They were right, and the bill was passed, but unfortunately for the prosperity of Honesdale, it was never possible to finance the construction of this railroad, but in 1867 the Erie took over the section of the "Jefferson" route between Hawley and Honesdale. The first train over this line was run July 13, 1868. All thought of completing the extension north to Starucca Creek was abandoned when, in 1869, the Delaware & Hudson Canal Company financed the building of the railroad southward from Starucca Creek through the Valley of the Lackawanna rather than down the Valley of the Lackawaxen. The local protests over this change in route, though loud, were of no avail, and the chances of the Lackawaxen Valley towns ever being on the Erie main line seem lost forever.

Additional improvements on the "Gravity" were begun in 1866 and continued through 1869. These were the final improvements of a major nature and left the railroad nearly in its final form. The most important improvement in this final work was the construction of a new "light" track down the mountain westward into Carbondale, giving a continuous down grade of eight miles. This section of track included the well-known "Shepherd's Crook." The track, after reaching an elevation of nineteen hundred and seven feet at Rixe's Gap, swung slightly southerly then, constantly dropping down, maintaining an even grade, the track turned north along the face of the mountain for a distance of a little over two miles, where at the "Shepherd's Crook" it turned to run abruptly south. To make this turn it was necessary to cut into the side of the mountain and then run out onto a high embankment, thus forming the famous loop which had a diameter of about four hundred feet. This new construction eliminated the need for lowering the light cars as was formerly done at the old planes on the west side of the mountain.

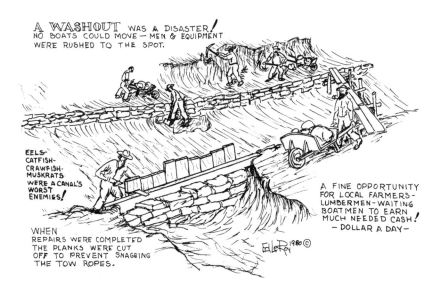

A WASHOUT WAS A DISASTER! NO BOATS COULD MOVE — MEN & EQUIPMENT WERE RUSHED TO THE SPOT.

EELS- CATFISH- CRAWFISH- MUSKRATS WERE A CANAL'S WORST ENEMIES!

A FINE OPPORTUNITY FOR LOCAL FARMERS- LUMBERMEN-WAITING BOATMEN TO EARN MUCH NEEDED CASH! — DOLLAR A DAY —

WHEN REPAIRS WERE COMPLETED THE PLANKS WERE CUT OFF TO PREVENT SNAGGING THE TOW ROPES.

This is probably an appropriate place to give a description of the manner of operating the "Gravity," before returning to the canal. As will be recalled, the original road consisted of parallel tracks at each plane, where each car being lowered counterbalanced one being raised; chains were used briefly, then unweildly hemp ropes, and finally iron wire cables. With the latter there were two cables for each single track plane. One of these was the hoisting cable, the other the tail rope, (or cable) which served to pull the hoisting cable back to the foot of the plane after each trip.

At the foot of each plane was a man whose duty it was to attach each train, or "trip," as it was called, to the hoisting rope. As each "trip" coasted into the foot of the plane, this man fastened the hook, at the end of the first car, to a short chain which was attached to the end of the hoisting rope. As soon as he had thus made the trip secure, he signalled the head of the plane by pulling on a bell wire and the cars were hauled away at a speed of about twenty miles per hour. Each "trip" consisted of five cars, each of five tons capacity.

Reaching the "knuckle" (the head of the plane) the brakeman, who rode each trip, unhooked the sling while the cars were still in motion and the cars then continued on under the force of their own inertia and gravity along the next "level" until the foot of the next plane was reached, and the process repeated until the end of the "trip" at Honesdale.

On the loaded track the descent between the summit and Waymart was so steep (about five hundred feet in two miles) that it was necessary to have machinery to lower the cars. Of course, here no power was required, merely a braking arrangement.

The brakes were located at the summit and were outwardly similar to the mechanism at the head of each powered plane. They consisted of a ten-foot iron drum upon which the ropes were wound and which was geared to a huge eight-bladed fan having a diameter of twelve feet. The fan itself served to retard considerably the speed of the descending cars but in addition around each drum was an iron band which could be tightened by a lever somewhat on the order of an automobile brake.

Regular passenger service was inaugurated over the Gravity railroad between Carbondale and Honesdale on April 5, 1877 and while the road never lost its activity as a coal carrier, it at once became a popular ride for summer tourists because of the scenic beauty of route over the Moosic Mountains. Although a picnic ground was furnished by the company at Fairview, the trains, like the canal, were not operated on Sundays.

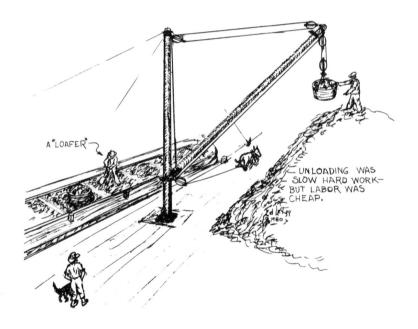

Progress dealt the canal another blow when in the fall of 1868 the D & H Company entered into a contract with the Erie Railroad which provided that that railroad should transport the D & H Coal to the

Hudson during the winter months when the canal was closed by ice. From that date on the D & H Company entered into new contracts or leases with numerous railroad companies expanding mostly northward into New York State and the New England states. This expansion and transformation took place so rapidly that after 1872 the company discontinued the publication of statistics on canal traffic. The last of these statistics from the annual report of 1872 is reproduced herewith.

*Statement of Tolls received on the Delaware and Hudson Canal and Railroad in each year since the completion of the Works.*

| | | |
|---|---|---|
| 1830..... ....$16,422 44 | 1845.. ......$25,880 92 | 1859........$ 311,597 79 |
| 1831.......... 20,554 64 | 1846........ 26,068 65 | 1860...... . 397,677 99 |
| 1832... ...... 28,717 51 | 1847 ....... 38,971 34 | 1861........ 367,953 56 |
| 1833.......... 37,004 58 | 1848........ 46,548 54 | 1862........ 316,376 97 |
| 1834.......... 36,946 07 | 1849. ....... 34,817 95 | 1863........ 954,822 67 |
| 1835.......... 41,976 82 | 1850........ 97,999 15 | 1864........ 1,213,570 46 |
| 1836.......... 45,154 73 | 1851.........158,441 96 | 1865........ 201,679 38 |
| 1837.......... 44,832 42 | 1852.........293,174 67 | 1866........ 118,482 95 |
| 1838.......... 40,328 38 | 1853.........378,479 83 | 1867........ 96,530 05 |
| 1839.......... 40,095 26 | 1854. ... ...587,349 52 | 1868........ 89,846 57 |
| 1840.......... 35,450 46 | 1855.........652,362 94 | 1869........ 110,172 86 |
| 1841....... 39,388 19 | 1856.........583,737 86 | 1870........ 110,258 25 |
| 1842........ 33,894 92 | 1857....... .435,198 44 | 1871.... ... 123,836 22 |
| 1843.......... 30,996 53 | 1858.........307,698 11 | 1872........ 109,786 75 |
| 1844...... ... 33,525 61 | | |

Total...................... $8,714,610 91

*Statement of Articles transported on the Delaware and Hudson Canal during the year 1872.*

| | Tons. |
|---|---|
| Merchandise and Provisions............................. ............ ..... | 15,944 |
| Plaster................................................ .................... | 349 |
| Cement and Cement-Stone........ ...................... ......... .... | 130,558 |
| Tanners' Bark.... ......................... ..... ............. ............... | 729 |
| Leather and Hides.............................................. ...... ......... | 1,690 |
| Stone, Brick and Lime............................................... | 51,521 |
| Iron-Ore, Pig-Iron and Sundries ...... .......................... ........ | 5,938 |
| Mill-Stone.............................................................. | 456 |
| Staves, Hoop-Poles and Lath.... ................. .................. | 4,584 |
| Manufactures of Wood.......... .................................... | 3,927 |
| Glass and Glass-Ware.................................. ................... | 1,010 |
| Bituminous Coal up Canal................................ ............... | 856 |
| | 217,562 |
| Cords of Wood.... ... ..... 20,913, reduced to tons.............. | 41,826 |
| Hemlock Shingles.......... .... 486,950, " " ... ............. | 244 |
| Ship Timber and R. R. Ties.... 49,503, " " ................ | 1,188 |

| | | | | | | |
|---|---|---|---|---|---|---|
| Hard Wood, board mea....... | 6,066,808, | " | " | ....... .... ... | 12,013 |
| Pine and Basswood " ....... | 789,363, | " | " | ............... | 1,184 |
| Hemlock, | " | ....... 9,575,769, | " | " | ............... | 16,758 |

|  |  |
|---|---|
| Promiscuous | 290,775 |
| Anthracite Coal | 1,409,628 |
| Total Tonnage in 1872....... .. | 1,700,403 |

While to the boatmen and lock tenders of 1872 no change in the attitude of the managers was apparent, it is strikingly obvious today, reviewing the company's records from year to year, that railroads had superceded the canal in their interests for from that year until the final abandonment of the canal, twenty-six years later there are only brief infrequent references to the canal. The D & H boatmen were by no means so fickle and no railroader ever had the affection for his calling that the average canaller, be he otherwise callous, had for his.

One of the greatest handicaps of any canal in competition with railroads is its inability to operate during the winter months for the merest film of ice made it impossible for the mules to move the boats. The Delaware and Hudson Canal, reaching as it did into the mountains of northeastern Pennsylvania was closed for five months of each year. Usually the boating season began during the early part of May and closed in early December. Another was the maximum speed of three miles per hour attained by the plodding mules and the time lost in passing through the locks.

Even had the mules been able to move the cumbersome, blunt-nosed canal boats at a faster pace, it could not have been permitted, for the wash thrown up by boats moving at a greater speed would have caused the canal banks to cave in. The only solution would have been concrete or masonry walls the full length of the canal. In the one hundred and eight miles of canal there were one hundred and six locks, each with an average lift of ten feet. The boats fitted into these locks like a hand in a glove and there was, of course, considerable time lost in getting the boats into the locks and in overcoming the inertia of the loaded boats. particularly when starting out of a lock, so that the actual work of lockage required the less time. The whole operation consumed no less than twelve minutes, actual lockage as low as six.

It is easily apparent that locks having a greater lift would take little or no more time to operate than those in use. Consequently, had the board of managers approved the construction. at High Falls, Neversink. Lackawaxan, and the Narrows. of new but fewer locks, each having a greater lift. the cost of operation and time of navigation would have been materially reduced, but as the railroads took more and more prestige away from the old waterway it became increasingly less practicable to make the improvements which might have given the canal a longer lease on life.

Two remaining disadvantages hampered the D & H: The Moosic Mountains remained a barrier between it and the mines, requiring the double handling of coal by means of the Gravity railroad. Finally, after traveling one hundred and eight miles to tidewater, the canal terminated but a few miles nearer the New York markets than was its starting point at Honesdale.

The last twenty-five years of operation of the canal were uneventful from the standpoint of change. The canal people themselves had settled down to the serious business of hauling coal and freight.

The following summary of the canal, while it is for the year 1880, will suffice for the ᶠᴵᴺᴬᴸ year of operation:

Locks: 107 (including double lock at Honesdale), 95 composite, 12 stone and cement masonry, 100 feet in length between gates 15 feet wide.

Feet of Lockage: 1086, including 58 feet at Neversink.

Weight Locks: 2 of stone and cement masonry.

Stop Locks: 2 stone masonry ends.

Guard Locks: 2, one masonry, one composite.

Aqueducts: 22, 4 wire suspension, 18 wood trunk. 2,000 lineal feet aqueduct superstructure.

Waste Weirs: 110—105 stone masonry, 5 timber and plank.

Canal Feeders: 14—2 wood, 12 earth trunk. Total 3½ miles.

Feeder dams: 16—4 stone masonry, 10 timber and plank. 2 stone and brush.

Drydocks: 2, leased, not operated by company. (There were numerous others of varying sizes privately owned.)

Bridges: 136 highway and farm bridges. 5 have wrought iron superstructure.

Tow path bridges: 37—1 crossing Lackawaxen at Honesdale. (5 span wrought iron.) 26 crossing aqueducts, 10 crossing feeders.

Reservoirs: 22.

Boats: 915 canal boats, 66 transfer boats, 3 freight line boats, 16 barges, 2 wrecking boats, 1 propeller boat and 1 dredging machine. In addition to these boats there were, of course, an uncounted number of boats which had been privately built.

THE locks on the D & H were numbered in order westward from Rondout to Lackawaxen and from Lackawaxen to Honesdale. For the most part the boatmen referred to the lock by some name which was derived from the proprietor or from some peculiar feature nearby. The most common names were: 1—Eddyville, 2 to 4—Creek Locks, 5—Milban's, 6—Websters, 7—Rosendale, 8-9—Lawrenceville, 10—Humphreys, 11—Cole's Basin, 12-14—Nigger Locks, 15-20—High Falls, 21—Alligerville, 22—Foleys, 23—Stony Kill, 24—Middleport, 25—Port Hickson, 26—Port Benjamin, 27—Bob Decker's, 28—Chris Ginniel's, 29—Shirley's,

30-31—Ellenville, 32—Sam Taylor's, 33—Youppy's, 34—Ostrander's, 35—Callahan's, 36—Penny's, 37—Mose Charles', 38—Louie Beardsley, 39—Joe McKane, 40—Hank Woods, 41—Jack McCarthy, 42—Bill Foster, 43—Bill Robinson, 44—Dan Hanion, 45—Enoch Rogers, 46—Huck Rogers, 47—Will Donnelly's, 48—Will Halstead's, 49—Wm. E. Rose's, 59—P. O. Callahan's, 51-55—Neversink, 56—Mineral Springs, 57—Butler's, 58-59—Mongaup, 60—Woolsley's, 61—Pa Gene Smith's, 62—Widow Kelly's, 63—Pond Eddy, 64—Squire Van Tuyler's, 65—Decker's, 66—Lambert's, 67—Handsome Eddy, 68—Barryville, Lower 69—Barryville, Upper, 70-71-72—Gilson's Locks.

Here the canal crossed the Delaware and Lackawaxen Rivers. The first three locks on the Lackawaxen were abandoned after the completion of the aqueducts. 4-5-6—Ridgeway's, 7—Joe Tague or Tinsmiths, 8—O'Donnell's, 9—Bishop's, 10—George Rowland's, 11—Saxon's or Larson's, 12—Westfall's, 13-14—Griswold's, 15—Jim Avery's, 16—Corkonian's or Chidesters, 17—Rodgers, 18—Jim Hanner's, 19—Abe Rowlands. 20—Pat Gannons, 21—Field Bend, 22—Mike Harrison's, 23—Jim Harrison's, 24—Frank Danniel's (Pat Harrison), 25—Poolpit, 26—Baisdens, 27—Carroll's (Billy O'Brien), 28—Rock Lock (Mike Connors), 29—Lower Hawley (Conklin's), 30—Upper Hawley (Hennessey's), 31—Wier's (O'Han's), 32—McKahill's, 33—White Mills, 34—Lonsome Lock (Dan Carroll), 35—Tom Whitaker's, 36—Chris Lane's (Miles Bishop), 37—Honesdale-Twin Locks.

It should be born in mind that no two such lists of names would be the same, but those given seem to have been the most common in the last years of the canal.

The accompanying reproduction of "Rules for Government of Lock Tenders", together with the "Rules, Regulations and By-Law", covered any contingency which might arise and were for the most part adhered to.

The lock tender was responsible for the level of the water in the sections of canal below his lock, regardless of the head of water above his lock. That was the responsibility of lock tender next above him. A certain amount of water passed through each time a lock was emptied, but, except in the dry seasons there was a continuous flow of water through the sluiceway which bypassed each lock.

In addition to the feeders, which drew water from the river, the canal was fed by brooks or springs which emptied into it. It was necessary to control the flow of this water through the erection of wasteweirs, usually opposite each brook or spring. By raising or lowering the planking at these wasteweirs, a proper boating head was maintained. A flow of water through the canal greater than a half mile per hour would have caused serious damage to the banks.

The operation of the locks became an art in itself and was accomplished quickly and efficiently. As has been pointed out locking through required less time than bringing the boat into or out of the lock. Originally the gates on all of the locks were the balance beam type, and each was operated independently by hand, but in 1865 the upper gates were replaced

# RULES FOR THE GOVERNMENT OF
# LOCK-TENDERS
## ON THE
# Delaware & Hudson Canal

## 1882          1882

**1. The Locks are to be closed between** the hours of 12 on Saturday night and 12 o'clock on Sunday night, and open for the passage of Boats and Floats during other hours, night or day, as directed by the officers on the Canal. One competent man is to be constantly in attendance at the Lock during the hours the Lock is directed to be opened for the passage of Boats, and be vigilant in enforcing the Rules, Regulations and By-Laws for the navigation of the canal, and facilitate the passage of Boats and Floats in a prompt, careful and business manner. The contractor for a Lock will be held liable for the faithful performances of any person he may employ as a Lock-Tender.

**2. No boat or Float is to be allowed** to pass a lock next after leaving a Collector's office without exhibiting a clearance or permit, which is to be retained by the Lock-Tender of the last Lock through which said Boat or Float is to pass, (unless it be a Lock next to a Collector's office,) which permit the Lock-Tender is to forward to the next Collector toward which the Boat or Float shall be progressing.—See Rules, Regulations and By-Laws.

**3. The Lock-Tenders are to Certify** the place of starting or loading of every Boat or Float which starts or takes any article on board, at or near the Locks in their charge, and not at any Collector's office; being particular to give the date, the name of the boat, the number of the Lock, and the place and distance above or below said Lock where the Boat or Float started or took any freight on board. Such certificate is to serve as a passport through the Locks that intervene between such Lock or place and the next Collector's office; but shall not serve as a pass through a Lock after said Boat or Float shall have passed a Collector's office.—See Rules, Regulations and By-Laws.

**4. The Paddle Gates are to be used** in the most careful manner and so as not to create injurious swells on levels between Locks. When there is a full head of water on the upper level, and the level below is not above a boating head, Boats may be swelled out of the Lock, but with the most economical use of water, and vigilant care. In every case when those in charge of a Boat neglect or refuse, when required, to make their horses draw a Boat out of a Lock promptly, without a swell from the paddles, such Boat must be reported to the proper officer, and the penalty rigidly exacted.

**5. Lock-Tenders are to make themselves** familiar with the "Rules, Regulations and By-Laws for Navigating the Canal," explain them to the Boatmen, and enforce them rigidly, in a kind and friendly manner, in all matters pertaining to the Locks. They will require every Boat or Float to be snubbed and held firmly by both bow and stern lines before opening a paddle gate. They are to keep careful watch of the Boat or Float, and not to open the paddles so fast as to set the craft against the Lock gates or endanger breaking the

lines when properly held, or so as to cause an unnecessary swell of water upon the levels to ground Boats lying near a Lock.—See Rules, Regulations and By-Laws.

**6. Lock-Tenders are to be vigilant** in their watch and not to permit any Boat or Float to pass their Locks without having a proper clearance or permit, and report immediately to the nearest Collector or Superintendent the master of any Boat or Float that shall discharge from on board any articles which are not entered on the permit or clearance, or in any manner attempting to defraud the Collector in the payment of tolls.—See Rules, Regulations and By-Laws.

**7. Lock-Tenders are not required** in all cases to examine the permits of Boats engaged in transporting Coal, unless they should have other Freight than Coal on board. But this is not to excuse the master of a Boat for not exhibiting his permit when it shall be demanded.

**8. Boats or Scows engaged in improving** or repairing the canal are to have the preference always in passing through Locks. When any Boat or Float does not improve the first opportunity to pass a Lock, and delays until another comes within locking distance, the last one shall have the preference in passing the Lock.—See Rules, Regulations and By-Laws.

**9. Lock-Tenders who by inattention** or neglect shall detain a Boat or Float, so as to incur the penalty of the Law, shall be dismissed and also be liable for such penalty and cost.—See Rules, Regulations and By-Laws.

**10. Lock-Tenders are strictly required to** keep the levels below the Locks under their charge at the height directed by the Superintendent or other officer of the Canal.

**11. Lock-Tenders are required to** keep their Locks in good order, the embankments clear from lumber or anything to prevent the free and clear passage on both sides of the Lock for the business of navigation; they are to watch the banks near their Locks, and when a breach is threatened, to take prompt measures to prevent it, and also to give the Superintendent or other officer prompt notice thereof, or of any breach that may have occurred. During the rains they are to be vigilant, and render all reasonable assistance to open waste weirs, to draw off water, or to protect the Canal banks and property of the Company as the case may be.

**12. When a breach or leak has occurred** so as to stop navigation, Lock-Tenders are to labor under the direction of the Superintendent or other officer, without extra compensation.

**13. No occupant of a Lock-House** will be allowed to sell Ardent Spirits under any circumstances.

**14. Lock-Tenders are expected to** take charge of any tools or other property which may be

left at or near their Locks, that belong to the Company, and keep the same safe until called for by the Superintendent or other officers of the Canal.

**15. Lock-Tenders are to keep the** Lamps and Lanterns properly cleaned and in good order, lighted up at all times during the hours of navigation, when it is so dark as to need them; and the Lock-Tender will be held accountable for any unnecessary waste of Oil, or its use for other purposes than directed for the Locks.

**16. Whenever Boats are detained** by a breach or otherwise, so as to collect together, Lock-Tenders are to take the numbers in the order as they arrive, and have them moored so as to maintain a free passage for Boats to pass them; and when they start, to let them pass the Lock in the same order as they came up, providing they shall be ready to improve their turn.—See Rules, Regulations and By-Laws.

**17. Lock-Tenders are to notice and** report immediately to some officer on the Canal any Boatman engaged in the Coal business, that shall sell or take off Coal from his Boat along the Canal without written permission from some authorized person. And no Lock-Tender will be allowed to take Coal from a Boat or burn Anthracite Coal without special permission.

**18. Lock-Tenders are to notice and** report without delay the Master of any Boat in the Coal business that is intoxicated, or otherwise incompetent to manage his Boat, to any Agent or Superintendent on the Canal, and are not to let any Boat that may be engaged in business for the Delaware and Hudson Canal Company pass through a Lock unless it has a competent crew of three male persons without written permission from an officer in the employment of the Company, and they are to report every Boat that may be engaged in other business which does not have such a crew.—See Rules, Regulations and By-Laws.

**19. A Liberal Reward will be paid** to any person that informs to the conviction of any Master or Crew of any Boat that breaks down any fence along the Canal, or has any fencing materials on board said Boat in violation of the "Rules, Regulations and By-Laws," for the navigation of said Canal.

**20. The foregoing Rules, together** with the general Rules, Regulations and By-Laws for the navigation of the Canal (a copy of which will be furnished them) are to be strictly adhered to, and to be enforced by Lock-Tenders, unless otherwise directed by some officer of the Delaware and Hudson Canal Company on the Canal for the time being; and they will be discharged immediately for negligence or non-compliance. Any penalty or damage that shall occur in consequence of their inattention or negligence will be deducted from their wages agreeable to an estimate of the same by an agent or Superintendent on the Canal for the time being.

## COE F. YOUNG, General Manager.

**Office of the Delaware & Hudson Canal Company,**
**HONESDALE, APRIL, 1882.**

Citizen Print. Honesdale

by drop gates, and hand operated machinery, by which both the upper and lower gates could be operated, was installed.

The drop gates were hinged at the bottom and so weighted that when the lock was full they could be allowed to drop backwards into the bed of the canal. With this gate down the boat slid over it into the lock. When the boat was safely snubbed the lock-tender, from his shanty over the lower gates, "cracked" the "paddles" of the lower gate (i. e., opened them slightly) and at the same time turned the winch which started the upper gate from its resting place. The current created by cracking the paddles was sufficient to cause the drop gate to rise into place without much further effort on his part. The winch was tightened and the dog (or ratchet) dropped into place on the cog, thus holding it securely. The paddles (they were called wickets on some canals) in the lower gate were opened fully and the water boiled out below the lock. These paddles were below the surface of the water, so as to cause as little erosion as possible. When the water within the lock thus reached the level of the water below the lock, the lower gates were opened and the boats passed on out. When there was an abundance of water, the lock-tender could speed up the passage of a boat by partly opening the paddles beneath the upper gate, thus causing a swell of water upon which the boat rode out of the lock, attaining full speed within a hundred feet.

The canal company owned half an acre or so of ground adjacent to each lock on which was built a house for the use of the contractor who was responsible for the operation of the lock. Often the operation of the lock was kept in the family but in many cases an outsider was hired as locktender. More often the contractor himself also ran a farm, did lumbering or quarrying or probably he ran a store.

## Maintenance Problems

Maintenance of a canal presents its own peculiar problems compared with which the problems of a railroad are trivial. It is one thing to dig a ditch and another to keep it filled with water and anyone who has ever seen the havoc caused by a single heavy summer downpour on a country road, not to mention a spring flood can appreciate the irresistible power of water. In the valley of the Neversink the builders of the D & H encountered porous, gravelly ground which would not hold water. During the first years this difficulty caused a great deal of annoyance until it was finally overcome by lining that entire section, sixteen miles, with clay.

The use of "sitting poles" or pikes was strictly forbidden for their sharp points, driven down into the bed of the canal, elevated as it was above the river, would be certain to puncture the lining and the smallest leak thus started soon became enlarged and if not repaired promptly, a washout was inevitable. As a precaution against such an occurrence, which could tie up the whole canal for days, the tow-path walker or watchman was an invaluable man. It was his duty to repair small leaks whenever possible. This was usually done by plugging the hole with stones or twisted straw or both. On top of this he rammed down some convenient sod or clay, probably tramping it down with his feet.

Poles of the boatman were by no means the only cause of such leaks, for eels, catfish, sometimes moles, and even crawfish were the cause but probably the greatest enemy were the muskrats who found the canal an ideal home. Liberal bounties offered for killing them seemed only to make those which remained more determined.

A leak which threatened to become a washout called for the attention of the emergency crew. Their scow was loaded with timber for piles and planks for coffer dams as well as wheel barrows, shovels, and all the necessary tools. These scows had the right of way over all other traffic and were easily reached by the D & H telegraph. Where a breach of washout had occurred, a temporary dam was built across the breach and the canal again placed in operation. This dam was built by driving piles and facing them with grooved planking which, when watersoaked, soon became watertight. Behind this dam the washed-out section was then rebuilt but the dam remained in place to give the new work time to settle and become watertight before being subjected to pressure.

With these physical handicaps to be overcome, and with the board of managers almost wholly absorbed in the great railroad expansion, the Delaware and Hudson Canal continued its useful life as a coal carrier until November 5, 1898, when boat number 1107 in command of Captain Frank Hensberger left Honesdale for Rondout.

The famous old "Gravity" was continued in operation until January 3, 1899, and on April 28 of that year the New York Legislature formally approved the abandonment of the canal in that State. On June 13, 1899 the entire canal with "all its franchises, rights and privileges" was sold to S. D. Coykendall, president of the Cornell Steamboat Company, for the sum of $10,000.

Thirty-five miles of the lower end of the canal were operated during 1899 for the purpose of handling local freight. One of the last boats to navigate this section was the "Ulster Queen"; another, probably the last of all, was captained by Chara Van Inwegen.

Early in 1899 the Delaware Valley and Kingston Railroad was charted for the expressed purpose of constructing a railroad over the route of the canal from Kingston to Lackawaxen, there to connect with the Pennsylvania Coal Company's road and thus deprive the Erie Railroad of that company's traffic. The Erie acting quickly to defeat this scheme, purchased outright the railroad property of the Pennsylvania Coal Company which it had operated under a lease agreement and as a further safeguard, bought up the right of way of the canal, thus preventing any competitor from building over a parallel route. This was the final disposition of the corpse of the old canal.

Most of the boats on the canal at the time of its abandonment were taken to Rondout or some convenient place for disposal and a great many were used for years as barges on the Hudson River. Some few were abandoned at various places along the canal where they slowly rotted, leaving their bones exposed; the last remnants of a once great enterprise.

SECTION 1. All boats not built agreeably to the model of the boats of the Delaware and Hudson Canal Company, or a pattern approved of by the agent of said Company, and all boats deemed by a superintendent or collector on the canal as being out of repair and in condition to sink or in any way obstruct the navigation of the canal, will be charged legal tolls, or may be prohibited from navigating the canal at the option of the Company made known by its Agent, Engineer, Superintendent or Collector, to the owner or Captain of such boat.

SEC. 2. Every boat shall have her name and the place where owned painted in letters not less than four inches in height on a permanent part of the boat, so as to be conspicuous from both sides of the canal which shall not be changed during the season of navigation without the consent in writing of an agent of the company. The boat shall be kept properly ironed and smoothed on the bottom so as not to catch lines when passing over them under a penalty of $5 for every violation of either of the requirements of this section.

SEC. 3. Every boat or float shall be towed by an efficient horse or horses, so as not to unnecessarily impede the passage of other boats or floats; shall have an orderly crew of at least three male persons, one of which shall be with and in charge of the horse or horses at all times when under way, and shall have a conspicuous light on the bow at all times when moving during the night, under a penalty of $5 for every violation of either of the requirements of this section.

SEC. 4. The crew of a boat or float shall remain with it all the time it may be passing through a lock; shall snub with both bow and stern lines and not let the boat or float go against the gates. They are not to open or shut the paddle gates, or in any way interfere with the lock gates without the permission of the lock tender; they shall hold their craft in an efficient manner so as not to impede the movements of the lock gates; they shall draw with their horse or horses in or out of the locks as the case may be. with proper despatch ; and comply with the directions of the lock-tender in regard to all matters pertaining to their passing through locks, and not in any way obstruct the passage or unreasonably hinder other boats or floats passing in, through or out of locks under a penalty of $5 for every violation of either of the provisions of this section, and be liable for all the damage which may accrue in consequence of such neglect or violation.

Sec. 5. All boats or floats when waiting for a passage through a lock shall lay on the berme side of the canal. unless otherwise directed by a lock-tender, and allow a clear passage for any boat or float that may be passing in or out of said lock. A boat or float below when the lock is empty or above when full if within 500 feet shall pass through such lock before another boat or float that may be on the opposite level unless otherwise directed by the lock-tender. No boat or float shall be laid up or moored at any time within 150 feet of a lock without permission of the lock-tender, and at no place on the line of the canal, so as to obstruct the free passage of other boats or floats, under a penalty of $10 for every violation of either of the provisions of this section. The person having charge of a boat or float shall when within a quarter of a mile of a lock blow a horn as a signal to the lock-tender, under a penalty of one dollar for every neglect thereof.

Sec. 6. No boat or float shall run alongside of or pass any other boat or float that may be within twenty rods of a lock towards which said boats or floats may be progressing without permission of the lock-tender ; and every boat or float which neglects to improve the first opportunity for passing a lock, shall lose its preference, and be subject to the directions of the lock-tender, under a penalty of $5 for every violation of either of the provisions of this section.

Sec. 7. No boats or floats shall be moored on the tow-path side of the canal, or any lading be taken on board from, or be discharged on the tow-path without special permission from an authorized person, in the employment of the Delaware and Hudson Canal Company, and then a competent person shall be on board to pass over lines and not impede in any way the passage of boats or floats. No boat or float shall be snubbed or fastened to the superstructure of the wire suspension aqueducts, or any bridge or protection railings along the canal, under a penalty of $10 for every violation of either of the provisions of this section, and a further liability for all damage that may accrue in consequence of such violation.

Sec. 8. When boats or crafts navigating the canal meet, not at a lock, those going from tide water shall keep the tow path side, and those going towards tide water shall drop their line and pass on the berme side, and both give every facility for passing. When any two boats passing from different directions approach a narrow place in the canal, which will not permit their passing each other, the boat going from the Hudson River shall stop at a suitable distance while the other shall pass such narrow place, under a penalty of $10 for every violation of either of the provisions of this section.

Sec. 9. No boat or craft shall pass along the canal at a faster rate than three miles an hour; but every person having charge of any boat or craft when overtaken by another, unless within twenty rods of a lock, shall drop his line and afford reasonable facility for such craft to pass by him, without reference to the rate they may be driving, under the penalty of $10 for every violation of either of the provisons of this section.

Sec. 10. Any person who shall obstruct the navigation of the canal by means of loading or unloading his vessels, or by misplacing or mismanaging the same, and shall not immediately, upon being requested by the lock-tender, or by any person incommoded by such obstruction, remove the same, shall subject himself to the penalty of $5 and the expenses necessary and requisite for removing such obstruction.

Sec. 11. Any person who shall obstruct the navigation of said canal by sinking any vessel, coal, stone or other substance to the bottom of the canal, or by placing such obstruction upon or against either of the banks of the said canal, shall forfeit and pay the sum of $20, and the expenses necessarily incurred in removing such obstruction, and failing to pay on demand, shall be prosecuted according to law.

Sec. 12. Any person who shall wantonly or unnecessarily waste the waters of said canal by opening any lock-gate, paddle-gate, or waste-wiers, or who shall maliciously injure the gates, locks, culverts, bridges, fences or other works of the same, or impair the free use of such locks, or other works, or damage or injure the same, shall forfeit and pay to the said company, four times the amount of damages by them sustained, together with the costs of suit to the utmost vigor of the law.

Sec. 13. Any person throwing the carcass of a dead animal or other putrid substance into the canal or any basin or feeder, or on any bank connected therewith shall forfeit and pay the sum of $5; one half of which shall be paid to the informer, after the same shall have been collected from the offender.

Sec. 14. Any person navigating the canal by means of setting poles or shafts, shall forfeit and pay the sum of $5 for every twenty miles so navigated, and in the same proportion for a greater or less distance; nor shall any setting poles or shafts, pointed with iron or other metal, be used or carried in any boat navigating said canal, under a penalty of $10.

Sec. 15. Any person who shall drive any wagon, carriage or other vehicle, or lead or drive any horse, mule or other cattle, upon the tow-path or berme bank of said canal except in going to or from their boats for the purpose of transportation upon the canal, shall forfeit and pay the sum of $5, and be liable to prosecution for trespass and all damages.

Sec. 16. Every person having charge of any boat or raft that shall take on board his boat or raft, or otherwise break down or destroy any fence or fencing materials belonging to the fences along the canal, or have any such fence rails, boards or materials on board his boat or raft, not properly entered on their permit or clearances as freight, shall forfeit and pay the sum of $5 for every violation of either of the provisions of this section, and be liable for all damages that may occur in consequence of such violation.

Sec. 17. Every person having charge of any boat or raft on said canal, shall make and furnish a full, detailed report of his cargo (exhibiting his bills of lading) to the most convenient collector at the commencement of the trip, giving a just account in writing signed by such person, (a duplicate of which he shall also sign in the Collector's office) containing a statement of the weight and description of all property on which toll is charged by the ton ; and of the number of articles on which toll is charged by the foot; together with the name of the boat and the name of the person having charge thereof, where and by whom owned, the place from which such property is brought, and where the same is to be landed ; and all other particulars according to the printed blanks in use along said canal ; and at his arrival at every subsequent Collector's office in the progress of his trip, it shall further be his duty to deliver to the Collectors a similar detailed list of all articles that may have been taken on board subsequent to his leaving the last Collector's office. Every such person offending against either of the provisions of this section, shall forfeit the sum of $25.

Sec. 18. In every case where, upon a critical examination the cargo of any boat or contents of any raft, navigating said canal, shall be found to be falsely represented, as being of less amount or consisting of articles of lower rate of toll, or be carried a greater distance than is set forth by the person having charge of such boat or raft, the person so offending shall forfeit and pay for every box, barrel, or other article not weighing more than 5 cwt. the sum of $5 ; and if weighing more, $20. And every such person so having charge of any boat or raft, who shall pass the Collector's office without paying the regularly assessed tolls upon such cargo, shall foreit and pay for every time he shall so pass by any such office, the sum of $20, over and above the tolls on such boat or raft.

Sec. 19. Every person having charge of a boat or raft transporting articles taken on and distributed along the canal, between the Collectors' offices, shall procure a certificate of the same from the tender of the first lock he may pass after taking such articles or freight on board ; and if he does not proceed to a Collector's office he shall leave such certificate with the tender of the last lock through which he passes under a penalty of $5, when the toll on such freight amounts to less than one dollar, and a penalty of $10 when the toll shall exceed one dollar for every violation of this section.

SEC. 20. Upon payment of the proper toll assessed upon any boat or cargo, or upon any raft, a clearance will be given to any person having charge thereof, which he is required to present at every Collector's office during his trip, and also to the tenders of the locks, when he will thereupon be allowed to pass. And such clearance is to be delivered to the Collector of the last office he shall pass in the course of his trip, and in lieu of which he will receive a permit for passing the subsequent locks, which permit he is to deliver to the tender of the last lock through which he passes under a penalty of $20 for every violation of either of the provisions of this section.

SEC. 21. In all cases when a violation of these Rules, Regulations and By-Laws has occurred, and penalties incurred remain unpaid, the boat or craft so violating them will be deemed liable, and may be detained under the direction of a collector or agent of said Company until full payment has been made, without reference to time, place, change of cargo, or of ownership of either boat or cargo so detained.

---

*No.* 916

*Del. & Hud. Canal Company's Collector's Office,*
Hawley, *Aug 29* 1860

Under and subject to the Rules, Regulations and By-Laws for the government of the Canal, Permit

Boat 531 *Jno. Gaffney*

Master, to pass to Eddyville, with cargo of 114 16

Tons, *Lump* & Coal, for Pa. C. Co.

Toll, 48 5-8 Cents per ton on account, $ 55,82

Draught, 60 —— ins. *O. J. Long* Col'r.

# TABLE OF DISTANCES

## ON THE

# DELAWARE & HUDSON CANAL,

### SHOWING ITS

**Divisions and Sections, Counties, Telegraph Calls, Numbers of Locks, &c., and the Location of Aqueducts, Feeders, Stop-Gates, Waste-Weirs, &c.**

ARRANGED FOR THE INFORMATION OF THE TELEGRAPH DEPARTMENT.  BY CHARLES PETERSEN, SUPERINTENDENT.

| NAMES OF PLACES | Telegraph Office Call | Miles from Honesdale | Miles from Eddyville | No. of Locks | County | Remarks |
|---|---|---|---|---|---|---|
| *HONESDALE | H | | 108 | 37 | | RR. Main Battery. Feeder. |
| LEONARDSVILLE | | 1 | 107 | 36 | | |
| HOLBERT'S BASIN | | 2 | 106 | 35 | | |
| BEARDSLEE'S BASIN | | 3 | 105 | | | Aqueduct |
| BEACH FLAT | | 4 | 104 | 34 | | |
| WHITE MILLS | CD | 5 | 103 | 33 | Wayne | RR |
| BRINK'S DAM | | 6 | 102 | 32 | | Feeder |
| DANIELS' | | 7 | 101 | 31 | | |
| NEWCASTLE | | 8 | 100 | | | |
| HAWLEY | HY | 9 | 99 | 29 30 | | RR |
| TUMBLEDAM ROCK | | 10 | 98 | 27 28 | | Feeder |
| POOLPIT | | 11 | 97 | 26 26 | | |
| PUNCH CAMP | | 12 | 96 | 24 | | |
| NARROWS | | 13 | 95 | 21 22 23 | | RR |
| SNYDER'S EDDY | | 14 | 04 | 19 20 | | Feeder |
| SHIMER'S EDDY | | 15 | 93 | 18 | | |
| BLUE EDDY | | 16 | 92 | 17 | | |
| MOUTH OF BLOOMING GROVE | | 17 | 91 | 16 | Pike | RR, |
| BLOOMING GROVE ISLAND | | 18 | 90 | 15 | | |
| CRISWOLD | GD | 19 | 89 | 13 14 | | RR Aqueduct |
| WESTFALL'N | | 20 | 88 | 11 12 | | RR |
| ROWLANDS | | 21 | 87 | 10 | | RR |
| PORT HOWARD | | 21 | 87 | 9 | | |
| LITTLE NARROWS | | 22 | 86 | 7 8 | | |
| RIDGWAY | | 23 | 85 | 4 5 6 | | |
| LACKAWAXEN | XN | 24 | 84 | | | RR. Aqueduct |
| DELAWARE AQUEDUCT | | 25 | 83 | 70 72 | | Delaware Feeder |
| STOP LOCK | | 26 | 82 | | | Four Mile Level |
| BEAVER BROOK | | 27 | 81 | | | |
| PANTHER BROOK | | 28 | 80 | | | Aqueduct |
| BARRYVILLE | B | 29 | 79 | 68 69 | | Stop Gate. Hauging Rock |
| MITCHIC | | 30 | 78 | | | |
| HANDSOME EDDY | | 31 | 77 | 67 | | Waste Weir |
| BUTTERMILK FALLS | | 32 | 76 | | | |
| CRAIGSVILLE | | 33 | 75 | 65 66 | Sullivan | |
| VAN TUYLE'S BASIN | | 34 | 74 | | | |
| VAN TUYLE'S BROOK | | 35 | 73 | 64 | | |
| POND EDDY | RM | 36 | 72 | 63 | | |
| DECKER'S DOCK | | 37 | 71 | | | |
| FISH CABIN | | 38 | 70 | 62 | | Shad Fishing |
| VAN AUKEN'S BRIDGE | | 39 | 69 | 61 | | |
| STAIRWAY BROOK | | 40 | 68 | 60 | | |
| DICKERSON'S EDDY | | 41 | 67 | | | |
| MONCAUP | MP | 42 | 66 | 58 59 | | Feeder. Aqueduct |
| BUTLER'S FALLS | | 43 | 65 | 57 | | |
| BOLTON BASIN | | 44 | 64 | | | |
| HONESVILLE | | 45 | 63 | | | |
| SPARROWBUSH | | 46 | 62 | | | |
| WESTFALL'S BASIN | | 47 | 61 | | | Stop Gate |
| *PORT JERVIS | SB | 48 | 60 | | | Twelve Mile Level |
| DEN CUDDEBACK'S | | 49 | 59 | | | Stop Gate |
| PINE WOODS | | 50 | 58 | | | |
| BIRD-NEST DOCK | | 51 | 57 | | | |
| HORNBECK'S CULVERT | | 52 | 56 | | | Waste Weirs |
| HUGUENOT | | 53 | 55 | | | |
| VAN ETTEN'S BRIDGE | | 54 | 54 | | | |
| FORT CLINTON | | 55 | 53 | 56 | | |
| NEVERSINK, AQ. | Q | 56 | 52 | 54 55 | | Neversink Feeder |
| CUDDEBACKVILLE | | 57 | 51 | | | Stop Gate |
| VAN INWEGEN'S BASIN | | 58 | 50 | | | |
| STAUNTON'S BASIN | | 59 | 49 | | | Stop Gate |
| WESTBROOKVILLE | WB | 60 | 48 | | | Aq't Yankee P'd Feeder |
| TUNNEL HILL | | 61 | 47 | | | Stop Gate |
| INDIAN SPRING | | 62 | 46 | | | |
| OAK BROOK | | 63 | 45 | | | Aqueduct |
| BROWN HAVEN | | 64 | 44 | | | Summit Level |
| MANERZA SMITH'S | | 65 | 43 | | | |
| GRAHAM'S DOCK | | 66 | 42 | | | Stop Gate |
| SNEED'S BASIN | | 67 | 41 | | | |
| *WURTSBORO | WS | 68 | 40 | | | Aqueduct. Stop Gate. |
| GUMAER'S BROOK | | 69 | 39 | | | Waste Weir. Stop Gate. |
| SWAMP BRIDGE | | 70 | 38 | | | |
| LOG HOUSE | | 71 | 37 | | | |
| BEATYSBURG | | 72 | 36 | | | |
| DAVIS | | 73 | 35 | 49 50 | | Summit. Waste Weir |
| PHILLIPSPORT | SO | 74 | 34 | 41 48 | | Tuppins's Bn. Feeder |
| COUNTY LINE | | 75 | 33 | 38 40 | | Aqueduct. Change Bridge. |
| PENNY'S BASIN | | 76 | 32 | 36 37 | | Feeder |
| JARED RITCHIE'S | | 77 | 31 | 34 35 | | |
| BRODHEAD'S BRICK-KILN | | 78 | 30 | 33 | | |
| CUTLER'S BASIN | | 79 | 29 | 32 | | |
| *ELLENVILLE | RF | 80 | 28 | 30 31 | | Mountain Brook Aqueduct |
| TERWILLIGER'S | | 81 | 27 | 28 29 | | Feeder |
| DECKER'S | | 82 | 26 | 27 | | |
| NAPANOCH | | 83 | 25 | | | Enderly's Basin |
| FORT BENJAMIN | | 84 | 24 | 26 | | Aqueduct |
| FORT HYSON | | 85 | 23 | 25 | | Rondout Creek Feeder, |
| BRUYAN'S BASIN | | 86 | 22 | | | Two Mile Level |
| MIDDLEP'T, (Kerhonkson,) | MI | 87 | 21 | 24 | | Dumond's Aq. Stony Kill. |
| MOUNTAIN BROOK | | 88 | 20 | | | Mountain Brook Aq. |
| C. P. HORNBECK'S | | 89 | 19 | | | |
| DAVID VERNOOY'S | | 90 | 18 | | | Four Mile Level |
| FORT JACKSON | | 91 | 17 | | | |
| STONY KILL | | 92 | 16 | 23 | | Aqueduct |
| FREELAND'S | | 93 | 15 | | | |
| JOHN S. DEPUY'S | | 94 | 14 | 22 | | Basin |
| ALLIGERVILLE | VI | 95 | 13 | 21 | Ulster | Peterskill Feeder & Aq't. |
| SNYDERVILLE | | 96 | 12 | | | |
| CLOVE CHURCH | | 97 | 11 | | | Four Mile Level |
| HASBROUCK'S | | 98 | 10 | | | |
| HIGH FALLS | HF | 99 | 9 | 12 20 | | Main Battery. Feeder. |
| COLE'S BASIN | | 100 | 8 | 10 11 | | |
| LAWRENCEVILLE | | 101 | 7 | 8 9 | | |
| ROSENDALE | RA | 102 | 6 | 7 | | |
| LE FEVER'S FALLS | | 103 | 5 | 6 | | Basin |
| HARDENBURG'S | | 104 | 4 | 5 | | Basin |
| CREEK LOCKS | CK | 105 | 3 | 2 4 | | |
| HORNBECK'S BRIDGE | | 106 | 2 | | | |
| GREENKILL | | 107 | 1 | | | |
| *EDDYVILLE | DE | 108 | | 1 | | Guard & Weigh Lock |
| RONDOUT,  D. & H. C. Co. | RN | | | | | |
| RONDOUT,  Private Office. | RD | | | | | |

* Collector's Office.  † Suspension Aqueduct.  Double Tow-path from Lock 12 to Lock 20.  ‡ Junction of Wallkill and Rondout Creeks.  § Boats pass three miles through Rondout Creek.

PENNSYLVANIA SECTION. LACKAWAXEN DIVISION

NEW-YORK SECTION. SECOND DIVISION

NEW-YORK SECTION. FIRST DIVISION

To most Captains a name for their boat was a matter of pride and importance, though some boats were known only by the canal company's number.

In their choice of names the imagination of the boatmen knew no bounds. They drew you every imaginable subject and among their favorites were flowers----(Rose, Sun Flower, Daisy), Trees - (The Oak, Pine Knot,) Birds - (The Eagle, The Lark, Linnet), The historical great - (Cleopatra, Noah, Columbus), Indians - (Pocahontas, Little Belt.) Some captains had no imagination at all (Model Scow, Premium Carrier, Marvin Merchant) and some just carried the owners name (E. Childs, Morgan Kerr), but every great American was remembered (George Washington, Henry Clay, Patrick Henry, General Jackson) and some showed their patriotism (The Patriot, Yankee Soldier, Victory), while the old soldiers liked to recall their campaigns (Vicksburg, Atietam).

The list which follows includes of course, only a very few of the many boat names and some of the captains:-

| | | | |
|---|---|---|---|
| Serf | Peter Hixon (Colored) | Mary Jane | Lorenzo Horton |
| Champion | Jonas Munson | Sir Isaac Newton | Chauncey Goodrich |
| Pontias | Isiah Davenport | The Bird | Zachariah Rosencrans |
| Brown Thrush | Alpheus Gallaway | The Bonny Bell | Bob Evans |
| Flying Fish | Alpheus Gallaway | Santa Claus | William S. Wood |
| The Cork | Charles Meddler | Nightingale | Edward Parliaman |
| The Ark | Darius Cudney | Matilda | Nicholas Serrine |
| Niagara | William H. Frantz | Sun of Wurtsboro | William St. Wood |
| Landscape | William A. French | Billy | Edward Piggott |
| The Banner | Joseph Munson | Nightingale | David Reynolds |
| George Washington | Ezekiel Cudney | Model Scow | Thomas Cornell |
| Look and See | Andries Van Wagonen | Hope | Peter P. Yaple |
| No License | Peter Van Wagonen | New World | Orlando Tutthill |
| Noah | Ebenizer Schoonmaker | Guide | William Murray |
| Tribune | Jackson Lambert | Bell Flower | Formerly ("No License") |
| Mermaid | Cornelius De Witt | Mill Boy | George W. Tuthill |
| Female Sailor | Joseph Snyder | | |
| Hard Times of Anyplace | Andrew Mesler | PACKET BOATS | |
| Old Bull | David Aber | Daniel Webster - Fashion - Orange-Luther Bradish | |

The following piece of poetry was written by a boatman who longed for the good old days on the "D&H":-

We left Honesdale one day in May, Jim Law gauged our boat,
Al Kimble had the left lock ready, for our boat to lower
We got our hay, oats and groceries at the guard lock, Where Pat Wier had his store,
Miles Bishop tended Chris Lane's lock, A man we were glad to meet.
"Tom"Colo made shade frames at Whitaker's And they were hard to beat.
Next was called the lonesome lock operated by Dan Correll.
Then to White Mills where Dorflingers made Americas's greatest crystal glass to sell.
On to McHales where "Mike" Hanlon went to school.
If you got hot at Hennessey's Josh DeWitt knew where to get you cool.
We were glad to spend the night at Hawley where three rivers run.
When you reached Pike County there was only one.
It was at Conklin's lock where "Loot" Howe's horse was taken from the stall.
Mike Connors tended Rock Lock, he was over six feet tall.
Billy O'Brien was at Corroll's lock and he was somewhat lame.
No matter what went on at Baisdens, Dan Vincinus smiled just the same.
Don't forget the Poolpit, you wouldn't if you could, that's where Mart Carlen sawed and
   sold his wood.
Then Frank Daniels, he was always big and fat.
Pat Harrison was the watchman but they called him "Shoot the Hat."
At the upper lock of Narrows, Jim Harrison was there, His cheeks were like two red apples
   to match his curly hair.
His brother Mike at the lower lock, would make the gate chain ring,
Every time a boat went up or down he went over to the spring.
We went through Pike County's biggest farm, they employed a dozen men.
The owner's proper name was Beck, but they called him "Field Ben."
Pat Gannon would say, "Come on loaded boat", the drivers would shout "Yay lock" just to get his goat.
Abe Rowland had a family he thought very dear.

Mike Shields was at Hanners selling Gluckenberger's beer. The canal below Rodgers' was rather wide
A low drop gate at Corkonian's where you had to close the slide.
We bought milk from Mrs. Avery a woman very kind.
Dan Cocks made brooms at Griswold's, although the man was blind.
There were two locks there, the upper and the lower. We were at Westfalls, a church, five houses and a store.
Do you remember Saxons, the hairy man? He lived at Barron all alone. He took the warts off your hand by
    rubbing them with a stone.
George Rowland, well known in Pike and Wayne. Billie Bishop left his father's lock to be a conductor
    on a train.
Next O'Donnels, the house on the bank all alone. Joe Tague tended tinsmith's lock all alone, and quarried
    all the stone.
Now we are at Ridgeways three locks. You can leave the tow-line slack when we go through the aqueduct,
    to cross the Lackawack.
We went another half mile, Tom Tierney, for some light boats had to wait.
Here we cross the Delaware and go into New York State.
The next three locks were on Charlie Gilson's beat. Pat Douney baked bread for him and mixed it with his feet
There were two locks at Barryville, a pretty little town.   When we got to "Handsome Eddy" Dan Lennehan
    locked us down.
Deckers then Lamberts, the next a man never known to smile.
Perhaps you know him - - - Squire Van Tyle?
We went through two miles, Hickory and Oak ridge.
Pond Eddy was the only two mile level that didn't have a bridge.
We went right through Carpenter's basin and slid down Widow Kelly's gate.
Pa Gene Smith had the first red Berkshire pigs raised in New York State.
At Woolsey's a man with few words to say. Two locks at Mongaup, then on our way.
(Butler's lock stands seventy feet above the river bed. We locked out on the twelve mile level, scooted along
(    the rocks with the Hawks Nest overhead.
(When we reached the Bolton Basin Mrs. Sompson was there when we arrived.
(That's where they had the big break in 1885.
(We have Sparrowbush and Yellow Stores, Port Jervis round the old mill turn.
(Them Pine Woods with plenty there to burn. Birds Nest Rocks, Green Basin, Sand Turn and Huguenot.
(At the Mineral Springs we had a drink. Then went up the Hill five locks, they were called Neversink.
The last lock wasn't very high and looked out on the summit. Thats where we got the pie.
Cudaback, Comfort's Basin, Van Engen's Brick Yard, Buttermilk Port Orange, Westbrookville.
You had to swing hard on the tiller so as not to drag 'Round Tunnel Hill.
We bought eggs and milk at McKewen's and at John Hamilton's I got off the boat to cook.
While the team went on alone to Craven's abutment below Overbrook.
Jim and Bobby Burns, Kernan's Halfway House and Shorty Brown.  Graham's Hickory Grove then John Murphy
    in the turn.
We went through Wurtsborough as level as can be. Going in I saw Pat McElroy on my way out Pat MacName.
Mike Rogan lived at the lead mines, so did Jime Malone.
At Summitville were Jim Gooney, Elmer Comeback, McKew's and Anthony O'Boyles homes.
P.O. Callahan, in his red underwear so tall. William E. Rose at the lock was a friend to all.
Phillipsport covered a big range, from the end of the summit to the Tow-path change.
Lock tenders were; Will Hallstead, W. Donnley, Henry Rogers, Enoch Rogers, Dan Hanion, Bill Robinson,
    Bill Foster, Jack McCarthy, Hank Woods, Joe McKenne.
All these men took some coal to warm their little coop, but Jack McCarthy took more than all the rest,
    because he had the biggest scoop.
John Upright, the same at all the other locks, could make a good lamp board or good feed box.
Louie Beardsley, they call this county line.
Next Lock was where Mose Clark lived, who painted up our sign.
Mrs. Callahan made our flag, headdress or anything we wished.
G. L. Ostrander made our hammock and nets to catch the fish. Mr. Yoppy had all the buildings painted white.
Jim Startup sold liniment and swore that it would kill a spavin in a night.
Two miles more to where Sam Taylor tended lock and Joe Quigley tended store.
Ellenville was a great manufacturing town and goods from far and near. Most everything was shipped by
    boat, even Culmers beer.
Shirleys Lock where the carpenter's shop stood by the road.
They built boats at Cantonville tho' they never carried a big load.
Chris Genniel came next and baseball he loved to play. Jack Comfort had a store at Robinson Decker's
    and was the first to make it pay.
Remember no hills below this lock.
Reformatory on the Barrom, they called it Napanock.
Port Ben dry dock, the store run by A. C. Cline.
Bob Drivers built boats at Port Hickson, the best along the line.
There were farming sections around Middleport and how the crops did grow.
We had three miles of good canal till we reached the fiddlers elbow.

The store at Port Jackson sold groceries and dry goods. Jacko sold hats while I bought mine from Mart Woods.
Scrub cedar grew plentiful around Foleys (Will Davis) and seldom seen was a large oak.
Everything was spick and span at Alligerville where there was no engine to give off smoke.
Some Captains said there was not four miles in the next level. But John Leonard the watchman said "yes".
Here I put the bone in the pot and got ready for the Highfall "mess".
There were five (6-7) locks at the collectors aqueduct and then a sharp felt turn.
Upon the porch in a big arm chair we saw our old friend Bill Hearn.
Next three were called Nigger Locks, for some reason I don't know why.
They loaded cement on the tow-path but we scooted right on by.
Coles Basin, then Humphrey's where Jonnie Herzog lost his wife.
Two locks at Lawrenceville where Bill Delaney lost his life.
Rosendale and Rocklock where America's great cement is made. Do you remember the spring at Websters
    over in the shade?
Milhams near Laughlins dinner sign. Now Creek Locks where they have the shortest level on the line.
Some thought the creek dangerous to go down, if the water was high. Ask Mrs. McGinnis (Margaret)
    She might know why.
When strange teams saw the hill at guard lock, they became somewhat afraid.
Now at Eddyville all coal boats were weighed.
Through the last lock we did go, George Debois, captain of the Pittston, would be waiting to take us
    in his tow.
To Rondout for our turn to wait when the cargo was discharged then would draw on freight.
On the D & H Canal our friends were many but the dollars they were few.
I'd be glad if we had the old times again, maybe its the same with you.

Boatmen employed on the D & H Canal - 1898

| | | | | |
|---|---|---|---|---|
| Aiken, John F. | Doolittle, Emmett | Jansen, Frederick | McCue, James | Shaffer, Charles |
| Agin, David | Donnelly, John | Jourdan, Charles | McCue, Michael | Shafer, Philip |
| | Dougherty, Daniel | Jordan, Thomas | McGinnis, Peter | Schroeder, Chris |
| Bennett, Philip | | | McNamee, Thomas | Smith, C. W. |
| Brown, George A. | Eck, William | Kelley, Michael | McGoway, Edward | Shanley, Thomas |
| Brnck, Nich. | Eck, Louis | Kelder, W. E. | McAndrew, Edward | Smith, Sidney |
| Burns, Jos. | Eck, Ferd. | Kearney, Peter | McClure, David | Startup, R. W. |
| Bell, John | Ecker, Peter J. | Kennedy, Patrick | McDermott, John | Sherry, Patrick |
| Bradford, W. H. | Ennis, James | Kelb, Fred | McGinnis, Lawrence | Sutton, John |
| Bracy, John | Evans, George | Kelb, Joseph Jr. | McAndrew, James | Stahl, George |
| Burger, David | | Kane, James | McFadden, James | Shafer, Jacob |
| Burns, Patrick | Fahey, William | Kane, William J. | McAliney, Patrick | Sahloff, Frederick |
| Broaders, Michael | Fitzgerald, James | Kallighan, Thomas | McCue, Patrick | Smith, Hiram |
| Burger, C. B. | Frantz, Adelbert | | | Sherman, Jos. |
| Butler, Dennis | Feeley, William | Lowery, Michael | Neimeyer, A. | Schycart, George |
| Baird, Riley | Finn, Henry | Landers, William H. | Neimeyer, William | Schleede, William |
| Burns, M. J. | Feeney, Barney | Landers, Charles | Naughton, Patrick | Stoehr, Henry |
| Burger, Elmer | Freer, Oliver | Lynch, John | | Solon, John Jr. |
| Bowen, John | Finan, John J. | Lowery, James J. | | Spellman, Patrick |
| | Freer, Joseph | Luby, John | O'Neill, Felix | Startup, Charles |
| Carey, Patrick | | Lerch, Andrew | O'Rourke, Patrick | |
| Cavanaugh, Daniel | Garrity, John | | Oulton, Martin | |
| Colo, Patrick | Galloway, Gov. | Murphy, Martin | O'Boyle, Anthony | Terwilliger, John A. |
| Coughlan, Patrick | Galloway, David | Murphy, Michael | Osterhoudt, J. H. | Terwilliger, Jonathan A. |
| Coyne, Philip | Grimes, Peter | Murphy, John | | Tierney, William |
| Carr, James, Sr. | Gabriel, George | Murphy, James | Purcell, Patrick | Turner, Nelson |
| Cummings, D. | Green, Increase | Martin, Patrick | Purcell, Hugh | Tucker, Bernard |
| Cummings, William | Gibbons, Patrick | Morrow, Charles | Pettibone, Jacob | Tucker, Thomas |
| Carney, Sylvester | Ganghan, Thomas | Murray, James J. | Pettibone, Joseph Jr. | Thornton, Joseph |
| Contant, R. P. | | Martin, Lewis | Powers, John | Thornton, John |
| Comfort, Richard | Harvey, John | Manning, William | Prophet, Robert | Thornton, James |
| Constant, Leonard | Hayes, Edward | Miller, Philip | | Thornton, George |
| Clark, James T. | Hamilton, James | Malone, Daniel | Quinn, Thomas | |
| | Hoffman, Peter | Milraney, Martin | | Updenbrow, D. |
| Dougherty, Hugh | Hoppy, William | Miller, Michael. | Rutledge, Hugh | |
| Donnelly, John | Hayes, R. H. | Mullen, John H. | Rose, John N. | Vicinnes, Fred |
| Dunn, Thomas | Hanrahan, Patrick | Moran, John | Rose, Joseph | |
| Deyo, Levi | Hardy, Daniel | Miller, John | Roosa, W. H. | Welch, Chris |
| Donahue, Michael | Hoffman, Ed. | Mullen, John. D. | Rafferty, Daniel | Woolsey, Richard |
| Dougherty, Robert | Hines, Patrick | Moran, Dennis | Rogan, M. J. | Wood, A. L. |
| Doughney, Iere. | Havey, Patrick | Markle, Arch | Reilly, Daniel | Wood, Charles |
| Dow, Thomas | Hotchkiss, E. G. | Madden, John | Reilly, Bernard | Weber, George K. |
| Donnelly, James | Hensberger, Frank | McCarty, Thomas | Reilly, Owen | Wissert, Fred |
| Delaney, William | Horan, John J. | McLaughlin, James, Jr, | Reilly, James | |
| | | | Reilly, William | |

93

# In Assembly,

## February 23, 1829.

[Brought in by Mr. BRADISH ]

## AN ACT

## To loan the credit of the State to the President, Managers and Company of the Delaware and Hudson Canal Company.

*The People of the State of New-York, represented in Senate and Assembly, do enact as follows :*

1 Section 1. The comptroller is hereby directed to issue, to the president,
2 managers and company of the Delaware and Hudson canal company, in
3 such sums as the said company may require, special certificates of stock to
4 the amount of five hundred thousand dollars, redeemable at any time after
5 the year 1849, at the pleasure of the state, and bearing an interest at the
6 rate of four and an half per cent per annum, payable quarterly at the office
7 of the said company in the city of New-York ; for the redemption of which
8 stock, and the due payment of the interest thereon, to the owners of such stock,
9 the faith and credit of the people of this state are hereby pledged.

1 § 2. The said stock shall be so issued by the comptroller, on the delivery
2 of the security herein after provided to be given to the people of this state,
3 by the said company, for the said loan of five hundred thousand dollars.

1 § 3. The said stock shall be made payable to the said corporation, or their
2 order, and may be transferred by the said corporation at their pleasure *but*
3 ~~the said stock shall, in all cases, be transferable only in person, or by attor-~~
4 ~~ney at the office of the said company in the city of New-York, in books to~~
5 ~~be provided for that purpose.~~

1 § 4. Whenever any holder of any certificates of such stock shall desire
2 to transfer, divide or consolidate the same, he shall be authorised to do so,
3 in the manner provided for by the fifth section of the act, entitled " an act to
4 loan the credit of the people of the state of New-York, to the president,
5 managers and company of the Delaware and Hudson Canal company, and
6 for other purposes," passed March 10, 1827.

1 § 5. For the purpose of completely securing the people of this state for
2 the responsibility incurred by the pledge of their credit, as aforesaid, the
3 comptroller, with the advice of the attorney-general, before he issues the
4 said stock, or any part thereof, shall receive from the said company, the like
5 security as is provided in the sixth section of the *last mentioned act, passed*
6 *[handwritten text]*

*[handwritten text]*

*Sir—*

The Hon. *W. L. Marcy, late comptroller, in his report in relation to the Delaware and Hudson Canal Company, having adverted to the Schuylkill and Lehigh coals, as the only anthracites that might compete, in our market, with the Lackawanock : and inquiries having been made of me, as to the probable consumption of this description of fuel, I deem it to be my duty to lay before you, some facts on both these points ; to which I beg leave to solicit your attentive consideration : and believing, as I do, that your conclusions will have an important bearing on the general interests and domestic comforts of a large portion of your fellow-citizens, and especially on our numerous and increasing manufactories, I trust I shall have your kind indulgence for this communication.*

I am with great respect,
Your obedient servant,

*President of the Delaware and Hudson Canal Company.*

*Extract of a letter from Messrs. I. & J. Townsend, to the Hon. W. L. Marcy, late comptroller, dated Albany, January 21st, 1829.*

" Your favor of the 20th January was duly received, asking our opinion as to the quality of Lackawanock coal. We have tried it in our furnace, and at the Troy iron and nail factory, and the foremen of both establishments prefer it for heating and melting iron, to the Lehigh or any other anthracite coal, which they have used. It ignites in much less time, and the same weight produces a better result.

" Twenty or more families in this city are using this coal, who all give it a most decided preference to either Lehigh or Schuylkill for the grate.

" From our experience in the use of this coal in the different manufactures of iron and nails, in which we are engaged, we give it as our most decided opinion, that the Lackawanock coal will be preferred to any other anthracite, for all manufacturing purposes."

*Extract of a letter from Capt. Elam Lynds, superintendent of the state prison, Sing-Sing, to S. M. Hopkins, Esq one of the commissioners, dated 26th January, 1829.*

" I received about a month since, five chaldrons of Lackawanock coal. It was put on the forge of one of our best blacksmiths, and be pronounced it the best coal we ever had. The smith's forge tests the purity of coal, perhaps, better than any other mode of burning it. We have also burned it under our steam boiler, and in the stoves.

" It burns freer, and is much more pure than either Schuylkill or Lehigh, and I have no doubt it will be found a better coal for all uses, than either of the other kinds."

*Extract of a letter from Lemuel Pomeroy, Esq. (manufacturing arms for the U. States,) to Messrs. I. & J. Town send, dated Pittsfield, February 10th, 1829.*

" The subject of Lackawanock coal is very important. The advantage which it possesses over the Lehigh, is very manifest in the furnace, where its heat is applied to the welding of musket barrels. I found that we could weld nearly double the number of barrels with the Lackawanock, that were welded with the Lehigh, and a ton of the former will produce much more heat."

In conversation with Messrs. Townsends, Mr. Pomeroy stated that with the Lehigh, his men welded from 6 to 8 gun barrels a day, with the Lackawanock 14.

*Extract of a letter from an iron manufacturer in New-York, dated 20th February.*

I have used five chaldrons of Lackawanock coal, and have no hesitation in pronouncing it the best kind of anthracite. It melts iron faster in a Cupola Furnace, than either Schuylkill or Lehigh. I have used it on the blacksmith's forge, and in the grate ; it ignites quick and gives a very strong heat ; it is free from slate and stone, which is not the case with either of the other coals.

Mr. Baldwin of Kingston reports that he uses anthracite coals exclusively in his furnace. That he has used Schuylkill, Lehigh and Lackawanock, and after repeated experiments of each kind by measure, he found that with Lackawanock, he melted his charge of about 700lbs. of iron in half an hour less, and made better metal.